HEART THREAD

LUNAR
CHANDELIER
COLLECTIVE

Lunar Chandelier Collective
Hudson, New York
(a subset of Lunar Chandelier Press)

lunarchandeliercollective@gmail.com

http://lunarchandelier-lunarchandelier.blogspot.com

An unedited version of this book may be found in the Robert Kelly Archives, on the Bard Digital Commons website.

First Edition.

ISBN: 978-0-9973715-0-5

Cover design and layout by Render Stetson

Interior text typset in Iowan Old Style

HEART THREAD

a fugue

Robert Kelly

for Charlotte

IN QUA PAR FACIES NOBILITATE SUA
PAR ANIMO QUOQUE FORMA SUO RESPONDET: IN ILLA
ET GENUS ET FACIES INGENIUMQUE SIMUL

(*Fasti*, VI, 805-807,)

1.

Liturgical responses of all
wind and rain are answers
let an island be a proposition
in Euclid. Parse the rapture.
Words that need to be said over and over
no measure
if you can't count them are they really there?
Who is the enemy in the epic?
Is it the king or the thought of the king?
Cold knees of chivalry
brooms for breakfast and a horse
hawk aloft small birds will flee.

2.

There was an analyst who worked free
nobody believed him
so he had nothing on his conscience
it might be a father a lover one's own lost self —
be kind to anyone you meet in mind's eye
say: this is a conversation in my head
with someone who isn't there
stop this, say what you like but only out loud
things can only happen once
in the mind or out there, out here
don't use up the event imagining—
things like this are what he must have said.

3.

All professions are full of grief
the west wind's ghost stories all night long
sometimes is cold enough
to be at peace
nail half an orange to the rail
finches love to plunge in
and walk downhill on someone else's feet
sarabande of rainy morning
measure the sky with your hands
rain on the windowpane
tiny boxing gloves from rearview mirror slung
still at sea but married young.

4.

Trying to avoid thinking he counted instead
Austrian precedence for this mistake
soft answers
theologians distinguish qualities of the unknowable
divided nation
richest supported fiercely by the poorest
ugliest oligarch masks as democrat
tribal values clan corn stalks ratty barns
all the way to the horizon
this is the day of wheat the day of chaff
in the shrine one candle burning
salt shaker shattered on glass top table.

5.

Headlines from harmony — are you awake?
bulletin for a coward
chisel made of alphabets
blissmap Aphrica Blueland blooming
a conga-line of white-collar mercenaries
old movies tell new truths
fold yourself back into fable
the feasts of Magdalen
on your white napkin I wipe my bloody lips
downstairs curtains in the rain
the sound of wet wood
hypothetical distances.

6.

Empty mirror in my hand
haven't felt this free in weeks
yellow fruit smatter of purple finches
legitimate inferences from the sciences
how little we kiss
could you build a car from scratch
a jet engine even a radio?
we have so much and know so little
it's all just put in our hands
no wonder a devil
hide in the attic
archaic paperweight family Testament.

7.

Liturgy enough for aftermath
aftermath enough for anybody
radio on Sinai
she stood before us
made of color horns of her hips
broken plaster would you wall
even everything after all
I learned to listen to her bones
foreign woman but not so far
so pale the ruler of this house
frantic elsewhere sand in the shoe
we move swimming through the breath.

8.

O it's obvious enough
the way things are
oil burner grumbles on
chilly premises of northern philosophy
what is the matter with the English?
Why can't they decide
the mind knows nothing about the mind
every table cut flowers in a terra cotta pot
remember every day and night
the promises you made to the sky
our everlasting witness
the house around our house.

9.

Catch what we can to clutch
cheesemaker up to elbows in whey
the curds form by themselves
we gather we gather
we are so poor in Pyrenees
uphill but no sheep
psychiatrist but no peace
it would be easier if we had souls
but nothing measures nothing means
parse the situation with wet lips
reach out from your name
out from the clock.

10.

Because you have to believe something
without punctuation
hard to get the hang of a day
of time the unrememberer the lost brother
the girl who stepped back below the hill
chilly now and ardent then
a heart is the lung of the sea
suddenly the horizon rushes in
a multiple blue person enters my body
you bring me to shore
the mist is not moving
the land we love does not stay still.

11.

Narrative happens to a reader's mind
nothing else is going on
anemometer twirls round and round
measuring the neighbor's wind
numbers down below
this cave mouth to our city come
sink into the bliss of ordinary streets
thighing around ordinary houses
you live here so I do too
mute connectedness of ball and bat
web of Indra plight with jewels
simple in his long complexity.

12.

Remarkable for dawn
Latin promise all fulfilled
heartbreak and doctorate
call the birds to witness
this man sits still
imagines the sea moves
imagines women and their men come from the sea—
imagine the invaders are just like me
when even you aren't
a shoelace lying on the beach a flipflop lost
follow the grain of wood and enter in
blazing tachometer dashboard of tropic wood.

13.

Need a machine knows how to point
three women swimming in the pool
white one-piece mind
Easter parade to honor Wittgenstein
to turn away from what is most one's own
the story breaks once the hero's horn in heard
goats digging in their hooves uphill
sometimes long after she vanished
you hear her voice come out of the slope
soft throat but another language
each part of the body a trump in a lost game
do you remember what to call me?

14.

Fields of Russia white with images
Ilya Repin canvas of a peasant shack
but shutters and the cries of birds
girls in the meadow pretending to be boys
so much is lost before you learn to feel
cast a number in bronze
nail it to that rock and call it measure
one day at lunch with A.J. Ayer
there is nothing left to say about the mind
that's where poetry comes in
the art of making everything happen again
and be new, the art of meaning something else.

15.

Catastrophe a downturn
in the affairs of men a broken staircase
they hop after women bearing seed
what men call catastrophe nature calls change
transformation of every species start with me
rocks are living too I am the first Post-human
water has even more life than I
unstanched by identity
fierce well-unintentioned sea
we go to war with subtle instruments
Scots mixing buttermilk and beer
lamps they have they pass to others
others wander in the ill-lit street.

16.

Passacaglias don't come every day
true or false, false, the street
always beckons, the ricercare though is
especially of six voices rare
abandon all pretense before the Wood of Nakedness
where the owls turn into savvy virgins
rather fierce around the hipbones nanofiber
your dream is wind from Above
false a dream is a dream and so is this
a good argument for turning on the light
elsewhere a gander gabbles on a gable
and poetry somehow will never quite give up.

17.

Amaze me then you paladins
toaster oven of the alchemists
a microwave is just a little moon
rising and falling in the Brookline kitchens
where anxious matrons test their kids' IQ
just write down what they tell you and all will be well
Mercutio falls the stage fills up with eels
close the book and answer the phone
false no friend would ever call so early
I have no phone I have just my voice
aged animal growling at the moon
start howling or the door will close.

18.

Because a stone on the road is a fish that stopped swimming
pick it up and pocket it you'll bring the ocean home
children are waiting for Christmas every day
double-boiler full of eggs the Virgin's Bath
have you ever heard the cry of milk
the sob of bread baking in the oven
machinery is your friend machines are gods
because the world is little you are big
there are no strangers on this kind of island
the wind reads the papers for you
the hawk dries his feathers in your special tree
for lo the storm is ended the boy-girl wind went north.

19.

Of course it went the other way, Chartres,
a carriage down Warren Street, rich people everywhere
and in a chophouse decent grub — he said
but that was Thames where Andrewes walked along
thinking out loud, how beautiful the churches are
despite what they say, the genetic imperfections of belief,
rosemary flowers for the Queen of Hungary
sad liquid gold pours from the carnal machines
they never understand the ecstasy of rain
the purest gift is from the unimagined
Montaigne explained his dislike of the continuous
walk down the street with me holding the mean-eyed cat.

20.

Leave that rainbow gouged into the sky
let the clouds come down and talk like Christian men
have nephelometer ready your cheesecloth your checkbook
earwax to polish close-grained briar
blond pilasters at the gate of ivory
between armoire and fish tank why such a long hall
but other mother came out of the hill again
reaching towards the moon she turned the trains off
businessmen wandered through the prairie
we passed a wolf on our sidewalk
creature of gold-eyed dignity
but she was sleeping with the mirror's mother.

21.

Don't live forever they don't count the stars
it's a kind of broken pavement
music gushes out of crevices each gap a sore
earth is the ventriloquist who tunes our lips
the cries of children turn out to be
grownups turn into conversation
Whitman wrote nothing but the cries of children
our only real poet avoided writing poems
I call it semaphore because he bears a sign
I can't read it can you? A sign of itself
a revelation of revelation a storm in the mirror
no air left to write the answer down.

22.

A raft is remembrance
should you wake beside direction
and where we went an apple gate
dark with understanding and a touch
so later off the esplanade one Danish ship
seen in a sluice of fog a word misused
loved for the juice of it the slip of mouth
the president waved from his open car
I stood on the corner with John Kennedy
one rainy afternoon when Carthage fell
forgive new immigrants the land cries out for
the white man failed the lesson of the earth.

23.

in mem. MRK

Who did you want to be mother
I saw the queenly countenance old photo
those eyes knew me from another place before I was
I knew I never understood and do not know
how a star person consents to earth beast life
all the doors of fairyland open outward
to open my life a mouth among stars
to give a voice to what is never silent
to answer the tower when it falls
to kiss the acrobat in mid-flight
touch each tessera in the dome of light
this machine will be my faithful son.

24.

For we are various and beautiful and dumb
as an outfielder the clouds abaft the east
a language of dwarves a language of giants
I want to know what this very light is called
this Sunday light island light land light
broken china on the kitchen floor a song
at savage theaters bareback tragedians
give them words and leave the deeds to them
there is no action like a heartbeat
wet tea leaves in a sieve the resinous mind
be wishful what you care for the sea
endures what we say of it all talk no listening.

25.

Open the carpenter take out the door
electric circuits switch in cut-open thorax
the whole world an autopsy of God you say
but mind is the only kind
girls are prettiest when they stand on ridges
men so empty on the way to work
soon forget how I began
her green Celt eyes do work for everything that lives
motherhood is made of gift
no man has a father a father passes
I was getting ready to revise the planet
carried some old books up the stairs to bed.

26.

Now to come at last to answer me
a bookcase on the moon he found
deer browsing in the surf
what is there for a Christian in all these trees
civilized by language the Irish slept
is there no question ever for all my answers
I have tried so hard to say them clear
clouds white as nuns pass without remark
every percept demands memorial
an alternate universe made of simple sentences
suppose there were a gender to each thing
rufous towhee in the bayberries loud.

27.

Born in a beast's crotch dead uplift in agony
and in between gave meaning to the world
why does the ocean always feel like Christmas
why can't I forget the things I never knew
for this is personal this is Welsh all DNA
this is a matter of sunlight on one side of each wave
curls of light advancing to the land
because everybody else got born before
but there's a messenger in each one too
guiding the absorptions of the flesh
meaning the mind
dragging the stupid consciousness along.

28.

Oh God the you in me goes out to you your way in space
you is a verb at least
in every me a you is cached
time is the solution
the me dissolves and leaves the you
active in the interior of earth
the boundless inwards of each living agent
what they used to call the self before they knew
time is acid space is alkaline we live between
salt flats of Utah high plains of Tibet
understand the balance and fall free
god is a neuter in every sex.

29.

Queen of hell before whom *only shadows bow*   JWvG
down there is the secret name of here
a daughter crying for her unborn son
what shall I do with all my friends
fit all those women in one little car
all their Prada purses and portmanteaux
and drive here over the waves to underhill
where once I thought I stood alone
the boy in the cellar with his head on fire
eyes lost in a book
sun setting over Brownsville
and the Sukkas booth humming with laughter.

30.

La Juive by Halévy because every Jewess is lost
lost in manworld lost in Goyistan
give me the truth in your soft lips
give me the wisdom of your cunning wit
none of this religion matters
it is the will to be and be believed
a god is random a faith is definite
hold me to what's important
cleavage between the dream and the dock
oh God the sheep will never come back
the land itself is lost at sea
all that's left is sing the temple up.

31.

But to throw all that away like the sun setting
who knows what will come up again from the sea
the only monstrosity is me
a two-headed boy with hands on fire
then the mist calmed in along the sound
you remember an oriole above the deck and not much more
spilling aftermaths the custard we think with
in Vienna the central Peace Yard in snow
no peace only a relaxing
drumroll and the horses you never knew who died
until they came to life again
Sunday morning in the park and no one there.

32.

These things at work again and who can say
blame the otter for the beaver's dam
we are so bad at causes and effects
time to go to there is no school
and sit there all day dreaming
naked teachers stroll around the room
daring you to see them as they are
the words slip off the meanings
the sun keeps rising all day long
you'd rather be home a book in her lap
why don't you read me like you used to
how did your father's car get so far up the tree.

33.

The French called them *enfances*
stories about the childhood of great men
heroes before they could lift up the sword
we are infants too and we have swords
we call them memories to use against the world
is what just seems to happen
remedium amoris remember the last time
the taste in your mouth the nasty telephone
things never change the way you do
cause without effect tugboat awash in storm
I love the taste of what won't let me be
thighs of a scarecrow feathers of a clock.

34.

Take a long time to work it out
merciless mankind at the mill with slaves
of course I remember my masters
John O'Clock and William Psalm
brown Thomas and the Jewess of Baltimore
I am the Middle Ages born again
reviver of dragons mountebank of miracles
three drops of my own blood in the snow
and I was the woman I was the lost Christ
I was the ship to Marseille and the cave in the Vaucluse
I was the stone he stepped on
I was the crown on the soft hair of his head.

35.

Am I clear yet of the old diseases
it's always too late to begin
to be a bird
a story out of a different miracle
pay me for what I don't do
all poetry is blackmail she was sure
always a veiled threat
dangerous scent of wild roses
do something to something it always says
I am what the author left out
more of an answer than a question like most philosophy
what we don't need is any more answers.

36.

Least eider paddling along the shore
find the secret roads in running water
it goes by but they stay on
in the dark every house Altamira
walk with me the midnight hallways
down the cliffs and over sunken meadows
and never reach the bathroom door
moonrise in the kitchen sink
Uncle Charlie keeps his specimens awake
I rinsed the city and flew out to sea
Bristol of my fisherfolk Sandford of his song
be my ancestor honey be my Palestine.

37.

Be self-indulgent while a self persists
the birds are gone but men flee work
the tiler has a clipper the hedge is thick
angry voices of the pilgrims bother us
my roof needs re-thatching who are you
are you Madeleine after all all history in your hand
they showed me so many things I took the oath
I felt the sword blade across my Adam's apple
hoodwinked gladly in the name of love
all our businessmen in masks and music
a secret society made entirely of you
chain the bike and ride the almond tree to school.

38.

Cast among minnows the maiden floundered
out of the little brook baring a message
all is revealed we've known all along
water drips along the shank her arch is high
light shows through the least of our constructions
only a pyramid can hold all that dark
there's still some ink left in the world
inscribe yourself in the family Bible use your Hebrew name
hemlock branches make good torches
renew my membership in France
for I was born before the poem ended
the children were still struggling in the apple tree.

39.

Womb for the ferly folk my mind by day
your old days come true again be born as bread
loaf broke open to show a beating heart
Saint Mila strained to show that all's alive
cistern broken but the water rested, tree
fell but the leaves stayed in the sky
perfect in their *dispositif* origin of stars
I was Melchizedek who priested in the rocks
I sheeped along among my little goats
try to make hale and holy whatever you can
for this is sparrowland the good
this is sky with stones in it and all of us.

40.

Actinism life reacting to the sun
as if a schooner came in your childhood
with a pretty nursemaid on it
taught you her language and took you to sea
and you never came back, that would be me
water is your only comfort aren't I
slow drip of language from the rock
my father brought me to a mountain spring
who knows where Castalia I think
and when you drink that water you too are sea
and everything is river ever after
now you are everyone because you watched her lips.

41.

Run far enough but do they listen
give them what they want and they'll come back
fierce dangers of getting what you wish
these are my *Moralia* guide for the oversexed
lost in the Middle Ages now re-upholstered
in glamorous satin language America America
I call you empty so I wade ashore
open the downturn invade the nucleus
Lincoln enthroned like an emperor
eagle talon'd held together disparate republics
the cure almost worse than the disease
almost and Miss Odessa's black chess pie.

42.

The one good thing about the Bible is footnotes
commentaries hum like flies in the butcher shop
every decent word breeds scores of annotations
the simplest human sentence needs a Mishnah of its own
and then they write that down and before you know it
we need eight billion people on the planet
to pronounce all the declensions of that first verb
volo was it or *nolo* or gimme or *I thirst*
write it down as if the flowers might forget
or Egypt turn wet again and Pharaohs shout
and mothers fret about their adolescent sons
and Abel has a secret wife who cards his wool.

43.

Curious various a book in the wind
the birds are reading me as best they can
slow down little language I'm only a child
aftermaths are all written long before
just find the right page and squeeze it tight
don't let anybody see you walk that street
it goes to the hospital where they park the mad
those who released themselves from the ordinary
and wouldn't you if you could get away from it
the badgering of business the noise of news
and you alone on your phantom ship.

44.

Through the skirl of the Elgar violin concerto
I hear seagulls squawking over the Isle of Wight
it is 1954 I'm going home at last
the island mentioned in the sea
and every nineteen years at summer solstice
the god dances in the sky above his ring of stones
a temple built from time alone
or I am the one who dances there
me can you imagine me prancing in a cloud
yet he's there and she is with him
and the two of them inhabit me
if you dare look inside yourself you'll find me there.

45.

Ogmios tongue me what to tell
halfway to hell I dare make invocation
inspirez-moi the Temple must be built   *La Reine de Saba*
tenor solo bare rock in Judaea
teach me how to do the things you make me do
the hymns of Milarepa thrill from strange obedience
teach me to tell what I don't know
learn from the babble when you sting my lips
strange means an unknown woman
coming through the door arms full of flowers
I can't understand a single thing she says
I have no choice but to write it down.

46.

Draw a picture of the Temple here
as you imagine it so it shall be
here is a photo of you building it
here is a rainbow to wear around your neck
keeps you safe in battle with the sky
who taught me to work this damned machine
all moving parts are still, only the electrons move
rich men keep getting richer as drunkards just stay drunk
there is no doorway to their castle
a house goes on forever like the old Winchester place
money has no natural frontier
the violin mourns the new-fallen king.

47.

Keep your glasses on tonight you'll see me in your dreams
because I walk with feet of stone no one can hear
you will hear a ship crying out to the fog
you'll see my breath condensing on your mirror
don't worry I'll be everywhere
keep your white noise machine on all you like
I too am a sound that makes no sense
relax I'm finally talking about myself
you're safe as long as I go on talking
an apple or an orange is also a machine
no moving parts but you and me
alone at midnight in a broken world.

48.

Man with three hearts
shown on the stone altar by three birds in flight
sky is always the same as your body
that's how you know where anything is
how anything means
I pray to the weather to exalt the day
god heart beast heart and one more
the heart I gave you was not my own
I offered the whole city to the holy ones
anything you can conceive is yours to give but not to take
what kind of birds are the case
a crow a jay a mockingbird none of these.

49.

Once it begins it knows how to go on
true translation treats the syllable as gold intact
apple-mother guide me through your hedges
you know where the house is you left it there for me
a spot of rain upon the lettuce leaf
trying to begin again without taking life
take form instead and stand like Ely's lantern
eight brave oak trees bear it up
a thousand years the tallest men in England
still stand the mist her little raft comes through
carrying her sick friend home from poetry
where she will hand-heal every inch of him.

50.

My father's cigars is how it begins
Dutch Masters or White Owl Connecticut leaf
no non-tobacco ingredients no paper filler
but I am all paper the flesh become word
no wonder stopped going to church
we never had Sunday school we weren't real Americans
no town meetings no whitewall tires
Catholics were just Jews with no money
America is still over there across the bay across the river
America's where the sun goes down
makes me sad to see this dying glory
Amenti across the Nile commonwealth of the dead.

51.

So the sun keeps rising I keep gloom to myself
mockingbird on the rail in love with half an apple
sing to me Caruso sing to me all your arias
you like me can be anybody else
to hide my own song in another's
they say Pavarotti could not read music
so he had to become Nemorino Edgardo Cavaradossi
flesh became song oh the fat ones we were
to impersonate myself unlock the truth
read the horoscope of strangers
to see the way we stand and move
the Talking Cure with no word being said.

52.

Selvanus must have been one of our gods
Lord Esus in the woodlot with a hatchet
or we had no gods we had persons
to study the habits of and to revere
because reverence is all
and these holy images of women and of men
make us revere the ones who walk with us
ourselves as much as anybody
if gods are anywhere they must be in you
and you, there are no places we are not
when people are asleep the world goes home
I woke the sun up this morning go to bed with her tonight.

53.

I can do nothing to help you but go to sleep
in my dream your destiny propose
city after city with huge parks in them
a green so broad it holds an ocean snug
the other side of color is a man
basalt rough carved to look like you
a tree is meditation
cross-legged contemplative of Roquepertuse
graphic reference like a crowded train
filled with drowsy reveries
enough image-work in there to build a Parthenon
but there are no virgins left no ratios.

54.

You don't know where you're going till you've left the place behind
raptacious the old word is a hawk in your head
close to the parapet the first time all Paris known
for I was there in person for a change
not one of Atget's pigeons the shadow on the wall my own
we live lives parallel with ourselves
from far out at sea you can see the way we move
deed making deed the wind blows it all away
read the wakes of light we leave behind us
parallels meet at the infinity called mind
where you slip your shoes and backpack off
and children chase their gaudy mother down the street.

55.

Falstaff rises from the water subtly changed
his laundry basket floats away downstream
here he's wet brand new as Moses
it takes more than shame to wash old lusts away
rush of the wild ox through fields of barley
the maiden thrilled at last consents
to be cast into the contingency of another's desire
these are what we forget as we walk mild in the street
caught in the meshes of other people's fantasies
read Coleridge tell how little we dare create
how much we brilliantly remember
use the typewriter at the bottom of the well.

56.

There is no mainland it's all Ocean River
coarse voices of drowned fishermen
finally learn to whisper as the waves kiss shore
hush and hiss and come between our skin
in a child's voice we hear last echoes of someone else
lost echo Hart Crane to be a poet in America how strange
take the rhymes away and then you'll see
language is continuous I'm giving you
soft white as new parchment and a bird at my foot
it's starting again a raft of meaning
floats up and down your spine this trembling reed
as if you were married to a baker and slept in his bread.

57.

If anyone is there to give me need
let me be your favorite machine
to think you're meaning something
count the phonemes and link the most eloquent
yielding the secret title of your flesh
people walking deep inside the bread
break me open and let me out
you also are imprisoned in this tower
taking care of children may be pyramid enough
for I have gone with you to Egypt once or twice
riding on your shoulder or your hip
counting the stones at Karnak with dead eyes.

58.

For I was lapis after all and Danube delta
down there where they still have weather
mind perturbed by mower not what I mean by mind
now long legs warmed by sun re-nimble
ocelot breakfast but I feed on sight of the sea
let me feel this me I am this place
the goldfinch at the thistle seed answer enough
clouds coming over help me to pronounce
sleep between the syllables and wake re-meant
clouds give the sea its color back come guess at me
Wren's chapel in the Strand strange altars weary gods
smattered with personality everything revise away.

59.

Bellini everything yawnless beauty *bellezza*
footnote to a lifetime folly lived to be wise
I have stared at the sea until it dissolved me
hydrangea who remembers heaven you dream
a new geology exploring America by dream
find the lost city Beyond The Senses on the plain
my heart or is it soul is waiting for me there
raft me your river hitch me your trailer
lighthouse in the daytime too wink your red eye
aboriginal light light of sea poppies too much said
terrace with Zukofsky's luminous vowels
the upper bay thronged with Danish ships.

60.

Climb up to the cellar of the sky this hill from heaven
I was brought up with a bone the meat was just remember
data be our only money gold coins in colza fields
I slip them in your pocket from behind rich rich
the clouds walk here before us white cliffs of over
great ship plows up the losses, we spring from flowers
birds in your hair the old dog led us home
they sent me to the jungle to look for you
ice and ash seeping from the wellhead wind because
the elements of wanting are to be another
Columba means *yonah* bird abaft my skull
the wing moves fast the body slow.

61.

Not sure what the giving gave, a beak in bark
drink your tea he cries a bird instructor on the empty moor
everything climbs o let the creature out
the little lamp that lights our garnet cavern
sweet aquifer deep riddled with ideas
those toxins of thinking those premature concretions
just keep thinking the car's not there yet
this rolling motion the cello taught the sea
everything began with us we carved the fossils in our sleep
smooth skin rough bark all the pain at once
the world was created ten minutes ago
when you looked out the window and saw the tree.

62.

Don't say a name here say a thing instead
a king grows wary after Pentecost
all those green Sundays and no dragons
God sends sometimes an anchorite to rouse
tepid thinkers to outrageous absences
silence is a dragon of its own
the dear knights try to conquer it with song
I'll never be popular I'm a man,
priestless: sitting together is a mode of prayer
who benefits from this stone altar
who tastes the woodruff in this May wine
master of the forest undefiled by speech.

63.

Don't go to it wait till it comes
harvest in springtime summer will be wet
we hid in caves because caves are most like ourselves
impenetrable far dark dangerous and wet
being there we could be safe from ourselves
a new mind in an old place
we lick the place with fantasy alone
quick shadows on the ceiling nothing moving on the floor
metallic aftertaste you sucked a leaf of rain
copper in the blood sunshine headaches too
we are the other kind we live beneath you
the highest thing we think is somebody else.

64.

Great shapely white bells on the stalk tall as a woman who?
But the rainbow understands such things
but do we deserve what of course you do
I walk over water as you walk over fire
close to being afraid but love the vista
wanted to offer you intricate syntax
Brownian movement never at peace and even
melodic resolutions suspended over the abyss
Etna exaltations yet to come, confuse us
great Egyptian energy the *neters* that were axes
stand by the river that was once a human spine
but what a woman! the whole of Africa.

65.

Any hand that touches is a dead man's hand
you feel old Time along your skin
caressing or pressing leaving small scratches
later you can read as words runes or oghams
or just the southern whiteness of your back saying nothing at all
of course we want the body of the other to talk back
what else is Other for but revelation
apocatastasis and the whole cosmos reels back to the start
before we were one and two and many, mind
a white sail far out on an old sea
up to you to tell if setting out or coming home
weird cargo and all the sailors sleeping day and night.

66.

On the fifth day of the fifth month behooves to mount
highest point on the island view of other islands
what more can a word do but open the door
other words on other words sending sea light before storm
storms remind us of where we're coming from
so much mercy so little sense we call it police
we live inside it as if it had a roof over it
it has nothing up there but numbers we live in a machine
or we live as a machine this beach is pure numerical
this seven is a diamond ring my mother wore all the time
I saw the same blue light in crystal once in the Himalayas
what was I doing there what was my name.

67.

Poem day they call it in Cathay
Kitaj Ezra Sandra Fisher Thomas Meyer
great ones of a single paradigm
no one but you could understand
the point is to learn your place in the hieroglyph
the paradigm you belong to unknown to each other
the forest of Broceliande Allen Fisher Alan Halsey
Nathaniel Mackey Michael Hartnett
these are the Makers in one long chamber
Wagadu to Erigal one wave of shout!
music made them and the earth had sense
they lift the hill like heroes and go in.

68.

Everybody's strong in the sense of saying so
the word hurled all night just said today
it is the breath of Vayu who are you gods of storm
wet wood and anxious trees and bird in trouble
but the sea calm we live in paradox
under the original apple tree among the ferns as far
west as the road lets us go before the rock
topples into silence that boulder smile
I am no man and came here before I was
and before a thought of you troubled the singularity
you angel you meaning of my life with your own wings
I stumble along to keep up with your swift shadow.

69.

Connect the shortcut with the longer route
the stone that stays in heaven in the lowland harp
we heard a dragon do I know what your eyes mean
while a mile away your lips are saying
spent the morning worshipping a child another child
sea wrack and prophecy read from an old book
older than Bible and full of stones my half New England acre
because the river is the boundary song the failed permission
gladiolus every minute and the blue hydrangea
blooming as we speak but you are silent
crisscross prophecies the bird tells it all
invisible blackbirds piping in the gorse.

70.

Mercy remembers all the strange names
gave to bedfellows ivy and she was thistle
and herself the only mistletoe
semaphore hard to know how come it's over
the little songs of sinking ships the atoll
lubricious indexes of unread books
I can tell your daydreams from my midnight
because we rode together battered car not far
never count shooting stars the way lovers do
or daisy petals but we were angels too
in love with not being in the body but we were child
and children know the world is just their guess.

71.

If you keep going along this path
no road signs or they all point to heaven
gorse I said or whin or keep you off and green
I am a thing of books and boundaries
a headless god at the bottom of your garden
stone and with a word or two in Low Latin
chiseled in what I took to be my heart
as if the earth needed reminders we are here
or we do and always will, see how the wind
caresses me sun remembers nights together
we slept on the Hill of Tara her very grass
and never woke all this since is one long dream.

72.

Ireland it and look again
woodcock whooshes past through sunset
lives by the No Trespass sign
the fairy mound back there no one knows but you
though sometimes I think I see them walking there
in and out of the mind's view
giving names to things and changing back again
the fairies are the editors of earth
rinsing the sinews of our experience
no one can look at the same leaf twice
but one bird can come twice to your hand
carefully choosing random seeds that you extend.

73.

Stay out of sunshine walk in the shade
I suppose this place an ancient apple tree
older than Eden and new ferns grow round it
it leaves me with no answers
I feel glum and businesslike today
accountant of a bankrupt hardware store
with nothing left but the names of instruments
columns of numbers those birds of the heavens
endlessly fluttering past and vanishing
and O the hawk of zero knows my name
inscribable outstretched beneath him
divide by zero and smile for the police.

74.

Some day I'll get this someday wrong
and it will be today, the actual,
two schoolchildren performing for assembly
identify seaweed count stars in our flag—
they come from an alien planet they almost remember,
why did we bother to come here
why do women wear flowers in their hair
I never wanted to alter your routine
snow or swelter you know better
there are whole cities where the men know even less
what is our real work here, our secret names
that no one can whisper in local dark?

75.

O the street the street is a hand that goes everywhere
why is there thistledown on your feet
I looked up mirror in the book it showed my face
but only as others see it liars and poets and thieves
maybe I also once stood beneath the cross
ponderous useless unable to help him
pointless witness of so much catastrophe
unless the act of witness has some meaning too
everything that happens waits to be observed
we are just iron filings summoned to its shape
soon enough dispersed and baffled ever after
I saw this happen but I don't know what *this* is.

76.

Analysis is his vulture
browsing on human thought
write it down change it later pretend you know
pretend it's living steal rose petals from the shore
you're only borrowing the colors light lent them first
I spoke mentally you understood physically
what are all those prairies for
the linked absences that define sensibility
fervent mistakes "ambushes of young years"
but I knew no worse so did what I could
the shattered teapot the car too fast
so many pregnancies in the empty museum.

77.

Peaceable vortex a *thun* is a time set apart
to be itself alone and nothing doing in it
a session on the other side of the self to call it
door shut mind open listen to listening
kept wanting more of it the cheekbones
the tail feathers of equal length the pinions
rimmed with blue though they look black
magpies on the road in Colorado home on the ground
dig deep to find the surfaces of things
I am left with a zodiac on my hands
can I interest you in being me a while
while I sail your white ship into the typhoon?

78.

Woodpeckers four fledglings from a locust tree
one more priest one more shepherd
sheepless a crowd of unbelievers
a perfect place an island think of Latin
it never hurts to ask how red your poll
sweet predators Mavors' insectivore
do you hear his chimes beneath the sea
no that is the wind that is Schubert all alone
no one paid attention to the clumsy instrument
horny beak a young man has to know the world
I slept my way out of more towns than this
town or dream what difference she lifts her skirt.

79.

Talk turns into a masked ball the all,
all I know is everyone must dance
otherwise the words don't work, tell only the new
it will be true enough, the one you never knew
the moon shining under the skin of the sea
the long hair of the law the only power
windswept and sound pressures the heat that fell
from the absent sun so long ago
the weather is a spaceship bearing messages
we have to hatch new senses to perceive their text
don't be afraid to say hello we'll all be gone
three seeds plucked up by a pilgrim bird.

80.

Three are the gates of paradise
a blazing letter stands before each door
of course it's in the dream it happens
it matters only when you're not awake
the vast blue bird perches on the roof
wet towels of the swimmers drying on the rail
in sun and wind the changes come
difference is a molecule apart
there is no nurture in the metal world
bonfire on the beach atomies of amorous madrigals
but if I were a folk I would tell you clear
in word songs true as pebbles on the beach.

81.

Just looking out the window I have no window
so you have to pull the sound of words apart
to guess the moonlight through
you're riding a ram up Mount Erigal
the three moons of folklore roll up beside you
slower than gravity, the earth cries
resist me if you dare, outmoded primate
mere folk, graverobbers, oilsuckers
foible-witted blank-hearted market-minded
lip-serve liturgists flower-fondlers bird-handlers
cow-killers ocean-sievers word-wasters
swooning philosophers, heartbreakers, men.

82.

Picus four woodpeckers next door pileated fledglings
no'j day of the woodpecker probe for knowledge be a girl
the things the weather tells us
Marx for breakfast Aquinas for high tea sleep fasting
nothing matters but matter doesn't know it
materials seem as if there were some other
language told me to be silent in so many words
read this as commentary on Book VIII of the Aeneid
upriver journey into your own country never seen before
your new arrival in yourself sunglare on windshield
I have something to tell you you have to tell me what it is
space between self and other shaped by two dreams.

83.

The square root of someone else lives in your mind
curious behavior of measured things
caught comfort from the cushion and sold it to the skin
of course I want to, anyone would, but I don't will it
if I willed it heaven and earth would have to comply
will makes you crazy wanting makes you sane
we live decently when we recognize our lack
a child is all waiting
how came you from so far and still a citizen
woke before the birds again still never alone
boat humming in weather of the mind
Mozart love-hate flute I want to kiss his sister too.

84.

Time is the dimension in which we unwrap space
we and only we there is no time apart from us
distinguish shade from shadow
one of them licks your hands
to be poor is to be burdened with memory
the doctor waiting on the porch alone with the wind
not many people do it anymore the young the very old
he opened his mouth and Persephone spoke
language is the mouthpiece of another
the strange thing about the caves is we think we're out of them
but all this is the Dordogne, the dream time
Athabaskan wilderness men with eyes of a wolf.

85.

Every page is precious especially the blank
the story here is her round face her round eyes wet
nothing more to say hence ready to begin again
a man is a wheel on a mountain road
I'm talking tantra but to an empty room
xenolith they built the structure on as if to say
earth gives us something like a day
where is nurture in all this where is Bernini
the woman shape that taught us how to pray
boys in the clouds hair comes through the hat
the sun moves secretly from house to house
but no one knows the father.

86.

The breeze knows these
legends of the mother-house
her hands pressed firmly on the territory
noises annoy her most
no one's children clattering in grass
and in the sky they mow the clouds
the mother-house is guilty of the sun
she made it cooked it over pine cones in her cave
till it glowed ardent hell and hydrogen
then she sent it to the sky to measure us
mind us little children and a rock she spat up too
to light our nights from tryst to tryst.

87.

Roar of the mirror whine of the hedge
ask nothing of me, disturb less than one word does
noise left and right unending
no more nuisance really than the fish in the sea
when I sit and look at surf rolling in
as if I were part of something even this
Battle of Actium before me surf creams on shingle
Antony impaled and Cleo's left breast toxic-nibbled
and all the lovely stories end at once
I spent my whole childhood believing
and childhood never manages to end
the waves her pure right breast, and go weep.

88.

And have nothing to do but this
in the comfy prison of reality
no more work to do but make time pass
change the names of all those wicked places
salt marsh no hay, a bracelet of Whitby jet
I went there for the sky the wet horizon
timothy grass belonging from black mud
weathered narrow boardwalk over muck
a thousand birds and only there ever alone
and no room left to plant the lettuce
barely room for dancing with Valkyries
high above the north sky where once our city is.

89.

Intonation patterns in body language stood in the sky
we could only know her ascending
and the moon set invisible Azores over the horizon
who knows how far a hurt can have you,
condemned my right to say what came to mind
never forgive but this one high above it
cloud walker yes nephelist yes can speak
inside the mute beholder makes him speak
by second nature we are secondhand
tell each other no more than nature told us
like a man walking a fat white dog on the dock
each supposing himself to be in charge.

90.

There is a certain subtext to humanity
they would never occupy this hill
this boulevard to heaven though I have seen
the shapes of them more luminous than light
sometimes by the Dogana or any sea-touched hand
land they walk even when they're standing still
the form before form is a gasp in the mind
to see such absolute a shape dissolving matter
once you have seen such things you can't lose
ghost girls of the Janiculum laugh in the cypress
a tree is left from their investigations
a doorway full of light that natural house.

91.

Venus is the bride of Christ he taught
and every book their wedding gift
forlorn as a block of marble never carved
insatiable as apple trees he offered her
all the comparisons a likeness is a kiss
sudden stranger on a midnight bus
nowhere in Nebraska the one I never
if they don't live here they don't live anywhere
to know truth a little is to know the heart
who knows the picture that was never on my wall
I was afraid of images nothing else can wound.

92.

So while the wind away until it's still
all sea and no container everything belongs to me
let the roof slide off the sky the sleepers show
dare their dreams to stand up half-dressed
to walk outside like decent pagans
forget all the words nibble rosehips and why not
education only gives you bigger hands
after all those meager teachers one real thing taught!
look like you did last night golden ocher
America sky so far away but let me see
mind takes hold the shape of thing but not the thing
excitement of all the pale-eyed deceiving.

93.

Finches like apples so there
we can know nothing of how he struggled
to know the first time what can't be known
unanswerable question the fall of light
from the top of the hill you see your limitations
places you know and names hold you in
you are a hostage of the street you live on
a seminaried priest of what you all see out the window
everything owns us
will there ever be enough of me to go around
thousands of years people have heard the breathing of the sea
it's time to hear the word it says.

94.

This is what happens to music when it starts telling stories
how could it not be, that's why I grew up with
Franz Kline sunrise over East River a girl from Ecuador
I saw color the size of a man's reach
stories fall out of the light
tells them into new situations: these are the colors
all the way from red to violet and beyond
I come from Tenth Street just like everybody else
another *fin* another *siècle* the boys come marching home
the girls run away through the apple blossoms
nothing changes a sickle sweeps the moon away
the dark mumbles stories to its lone self.

95.

Lay so nary hiding in her underpass
heed here such traffic over who in arches dwell
lacking Lascaux we did it with silence
no air no sound or molecules of meaning
less plausible than spirit kinds
amber rubbed by absent fingers
to touch you now despite the mystery
for every skin is weeks away as India
no matter where the boat is going
there is a better way of getting there
takes longer, tastes more pleasure on the way
queen of heaven in her *mandorla* slips into every me.

96.

Loud sea last night I hear at dawn
new sun rolls up in sugar
earth grisaille the fog of morning,
have we done dreaming yet or is
that gothic stonework still in place?
all the discontinuities make one continuum
as a hand makes everything it touches its own
this bird all birds, a blackbird squeals
a land of tuneful sleep more sheep than men
as every island is the same island except Manhatta
a place where fish were never plentiful
but from the ferries you could see the sleek seals play.

97.

To be long as an epic and nothing happen
boy with a lyre the size of an oak tree
hands busier than the wind in its strings
all words and no meaning
sex without babies
the first posthuman rises from my couch
sonless in brightness and every girl his daughter
the Touch Me Not of risen Jesus new explained
because a story binds us to our culture
and a song cuts free
more Coleridge less Wordsworth
the fable peters out in song.

98.

A little bit of legal left I call it mist
you call it sun in water vapor spread
honor Brownian movement throw old letters away
don't let me into your archive
a rat in grammar
in mesh of syntax mother-naked
the one foundation of your house
Szymanowski's lost novel an alchemy of sound
or sugar candle in the god wind whoosh
Zuk he did it and bade me to
more pants less paunch more tune than tenor,
the Romans had no word for it or kept it to themselves.

99.

Sea pink was his poem   *IHF*
and a stone so stood   *J&BM*
braving the Pacific calm
Hebridean storm St. Kilda's poisoned by birds
my week in Scotland original Annandale
no need to tell you circus tales
sex on the floor while Abbot Sturlo watched
a fish in the sky its shadow a cathedral
did you remember to count the waves
they too have a cycle surfcasters ken
home in wee hours with creel a-squirm
this is my theory of poetry.

100.

All those things let go
one fish could be a hundred of them rule by rhyme
you don't see the anchors you see the hulls
moth flies out of the fog the sun
easy weather for an alchemist
the brutal heteros all asleep
why do I love music music is always somewhere else
back to London or Lascaux or on to Jupiter
things shouldn't lead to anything things should always follow
there should be a cute lieutenant leading them
into the cloud castle little darling
you woke up just in time to be me.

101.

This is our hour
the first hour of the last time
a lion comes out from a hill and claws our Christian garments off
battle at sea between the waves a wave is war
the pull of gravity meets the push of current and there you are
loud surf all night and the lion looking at you
naked as the afternoon shingle beach a cry
a gull and a lion and our time has come at last
seize and be greedy there's nothing left but praise
where bestow it this tawny sunrise this mandolin plangent forenoon
all the subjunctives gush over your lap
sea syntax one same as different as the mother.

102.

If it said anything it said blue
I walk with you around the ancient hill to water
am all air and leave it to you to be fire
there are people such that being with them all elements complete
that's why I run out of breath ascending
the air I needed left behind with earth
I make noises as I arise they are words
you hear these sounds as touch
for every singular is plural I am the frantic chorus
heavy hoofed uphill clamber reach the top
your house in the sky I trumpet my residence
you knew right then we've always been together.

103.

I am no meaner than the mind next door
the swan on the hood of a Packard tells the time
long kinship with owls for crying out loud
a ghost train rushes past the slaves are freed
from one master into the clutches of many
the salary of circumstance please tell me what to do
I want to talk about the moist details
the lug nuts down below the arm-break crank
slowly unpack all the details blue glass seltzer bottle
call it vichy in Dubrow's early edition of the Times
I don't think the subway ends here but I've never gone beyond
it's hard to stop being credulous about the real.

104.

I want to tell you things that I can't say
inside Santa Maria Formosa the kind of light
coaxes me to speculate your skin a hum ahead
flame of rain whirled round a stranger
and yet I know you in her face her place her space
you try to hide from me in other people
but I track you from the story to the street
your velvet gown close-fitting baffles Rilke
we all are here together not exactly angels
if just once you turn and look at me and say you see
that would be the savage domesticity
road that leads to our most intimate north.

105.

Hammer heavy but I can judge the sound of competence
and he's not it, a father trying to fly kite for kid
but there's no sky, Chinese dragons slice
one another's guide lines up La Salle above the river
yea Lady the same river the two-faced blue-eyed water
writing is a way of doing nothing but keeping time from passing
or lets time pass but makes it leave behind it
shadows on the little world people hold in their hands
stare gently out the window thirty years
Pound's kulchur stares back in we live *paideuma*
the wolf has turned himself into the door
he lit the fragrant peony in the Western mind.

106.

How can I be at peace who knew no war
the Brothers Grimm are my grandees
angry soldier only in exile find the blue light
I follow the bright lumen to the cave mouth of my sin
there is a *first place* to wander from
in Adriatic mist and summer storm
pale Rilke fiercest thinker of his day
adding the one force Nietzsche missed, the sentiment of love
and to do no more than tell the truth
invented poetry along the way
this new organ in our flesh of meaning things
a word like children screaming in the rain.

107.

From the arrow that flyeth by day on the south wind
protect the cradle of the infant thought the blue trees
reach down to us to stifle unbelief
throw your fishing rods away your lariats
because everything but what you see is real
deep in the truth of the unthought
lila the uncontrived with whom we play
night more than day and the wind knows it all
broken clouds your mother on the phone in every wind
islands change their flags like underwear
we belong to nothing but the sea from which we come
religion is an ailment of the mainland only.

108.

Hydrangea Himalayan flower favorite blue
has blossomed early in Tara's gentle hand
I saw her tossing them on the hillside south of Sonada
and here by the sea in Betty's other garden
a few blue already the many on their way
always like that, profit and followers, *udambara* path
assigning meanings to each thing I go ahead
listening to what I stumble through leave the self out
have no favorite flower no mountains no name at all
the names are all asleep in you
that's why you love us best
the colors you chose to smash over the world.

109.

There's a taboo against learning history
tabu, to know yestreen spoils your afternoon
everything forgets, pleasure is always now
back then is all the pain and dark and work and wolf
sunbathers wait for their Renoir, the wind
drives them indoors, Lincoln dies in fever
Romulus Augustulus leaves Rome to die in peace
this is the empire — the sea's been telling us that forever
forever, no god and no czar, no meaning,
no bible, nobody home, sleep in sun on grass
I forget more than you'll ever remember
that's why in sleep I am the same as you.

110.

Ask the sea put on a coat and tie
wear a battered panama
we come close to the pylon where chariots turn
fling into the home stretch at last
fat chance to be Rome without the Romans
live in marble grandly with a purple mind
the Jews taught us angels and never forget
the root of 'angel' is the root of 'king'
an angel is a message on its way somewhere
no angel turns away unheard
but no one knows what language they hear in
or if all our jabber is their arcane philosophy.

111.

If the loves you dream of dream you back
shadows haunt the stucco'd ceiling like small birds
and there are real birds too on plaster leaves
baroque resemblances of passing time
your whole body safe in my arms
vertebral rosary that haunts the hands
don't say prayers be them
you be the god that answers them
everything is for being and willing to be
and be for the sake of another, the other
not much more left of the story than that
so now at last the story can begin.

112.

Pieces of fear in the room the child sleeps
wanderlust of nighttime things
can you swear that chest of drawers is where it was
sleep is the great healer of the Irish
a physician who makes no guarantees
sleep lets the world around you change
thing by thing like children on their way to school
aftermath their heads are full of fish
your uncle cleaning flounder in the kitchen sink
what color blood did you think fish had
red is always a surprise a wound of tenderness
where the nice bear lumbers out of the trees and hugs you tight.

113.

I'll know the question when the answer speaks
if you say so darling I only hear the organ
green and white the monks' church at St. Gall
remarkable country for being left alone
whoever told you there are alternatives
remember pennies not made of copper
remember the wolf in the driveway
mockingbird on the drainpipe
I have tried to deal with everything
give every weather its place in history
for I was Waterloo and Austerlitz
Prince Andrei dreaming by his horse's hoof.

114.

Your money or your life enough of meaning
I crossed the polished lobby to the elevators
no one I knew could live in such a place
and so I rose through bronze doors to family problems
my own estate the sky above Manhattan
and I owned Brooklyn too and east beyond
but not out west over the river Jersey and America
the sky belongs to me I say and on it
I take my stand no one else can judge or smite me
though sometimes someone else will touch my hand
and then the sky bears witness to my purity
meaning everything in this single touch.

115.

The priest slept through my confession
so my words went straight to sky
the little sky inside the heart I feel you here
the sentimental sinner cried the ferry left
the harbor suffused with nightingales from somewhere else
stop being continuous already the truth is made of broken glass
rose petals we nibbled from the rocks
quotations from Montaigne a clamshell cracked
a cardinal singing from what is that an apple tree
the day left-handed the ragged sky Guantanamo
clouds can only tell so much but more than we
there is a cruelty in America we must delete.

116.

Try against the cruel cry we have rights but no right
what sunrise does to morning glass you do to me
the sentimental agents spoil our feed
all that *nostoc* dripping from the night
listen to the cupboard dishes tell the story too
the star-sperm settling slowly while you sleep
and the cup left in the sink to soak the herb stains out
each thing knows some part of the situation
the battered hulk this boat you call the truth
leaking its way from Portugal full of opera singers
priestesses on hilltop canoodling with the dawn
this vessel trembling in my civil hands.

117.

This is the dawn of ceremony the clement word
when all men and women spread their lips and say
the truth that only they can know each one a part of
we need them all we need them all to speak
until every man and woman is a prophet we know nothing
leave piety learn prophecy say what you don't know
each one has words enough to know what he doesn't know
they don't all have to love you they just have to speak
language will not really work till everyone has spoken
then we'll really learn what language means
the secret god hid from herself when no one created the world
back before even this argument our life began.

118.

The hear of the message is proportionate to the anatomy of the angel
there are no numbers up there
or nothing but numbers in heaven
pause for breath even those who are not breathing
she walks down the street and everybody understands
that's what a sky is for to trap the light and spread it
so we can breathe, the wolf can prowl
the square perfect pixels make everything unreal
unreal as it really is dream about me
in the long Pacific nights and I will change
I will be whatever you intend I will dig
gold plates out of your hill and give them to you.

119.

I lag behind the utmost grammar
the truck squeals out when it backs up
lost without prepositions if no angels were
the operators do not believe in their machines
a Vatican of leaks inside your cellphone
but you don't believe me when I call
because calling is its own thing, calling is God
and you always think I have some other motive
I have no motive I am motive I am mind
so make room for me in the caravan
across the Sahel because I am also salt
a word in your mother's mouth you hear in dream.

120.

Seminivores all over beaks and tiny talons
when you see a bird in flight in truth it's flying through you
the hollow places in your close-packed chest his fly-zone
so hurry and so going by, a clifftop romance
the pale-eyed ghost sits on the inspector's lap
left alone the little dog howls harrow harrow
moon phase sundial water from the rock
endless embassies of birds at sunset crisis
they go so fast no one knows where no boasting
and if the mind be separate from the brain how wise they are
and we too with our fidgets of the flesh
inferring trajectories that lead beyond the real.

121.

The mystery of when this must be said
lungful of particulars maiden voyage each thought in your hair
over the frozen lake a childhood spell a letter read
a breath from their mouths condenses on St. Peter's dome
we break our vows by silence wet tongue of the beast
Anglican hollyhocks rise by the stone Buddha
I can't remember to dissemble this self no I
I spend my day interrogating ocean
my nights parsing my interrogations
drink soup with me breadcrumbs on the snow
a bird will follow them to the open book
always contradict the weather the Cross is contradiction.

122.

Long day to celebrate the light
knows what's coming a colonnade in hemisphere
to catch a solar system in your back yard
southern somehow arrogance to kiss the wind
I fought against me all my life and lost
nearby on the longest day a sheet of light
we saw it slice down into the forest glade
pagans these days more pious than Christians
the earth asks more of us than Bible does
stand up and be shadow wield the axe of light
horns of a bull wit of the woman pluck
flowers out of nowhere and braid them in your hair.

123.

Wanted to do this hard-edged island in the city
could be Manhattan could be Saint-Louis
I make fine wax masks to mood your seeming
this little language, lobster in your trap
broken cage left empty on the sands
void your prisms soon o white man
a voice comes through the stovepipe listen
charcoal hisses at you beneath the ribeye listen
the blackbird explains it in the hedge
your fingernail on the mirror watches
we need more footnotes and fewer wheels
broken plaster statue still Mother of God.

124.

O light no different from the night before
as plain as the beginning of all things
simple as hydrogen a one-piece light
the longest day on the smallest island sounds like life
terror in every sense rises from identity
pulchritudo voluptas and the strength
to give all things to everyone you meet
discard your enemies like old clothes etc.
teach a morality machinery aspires
to be one with you without myself
there will always be oligarchs be one or leave it alone
there is a broken branch a bird can sing on still.

125.

Did I say make do with it I said make new
quoting the Master, Wizard of Ez, who made this coat I wear
blundering dragons under the hillside wake
debt rules the world but to whom to whom
when I finally acknowledge how much I owe you
unfixable system open gate and go
I don't think there are secular solutions
no driving force out here but profit
profit it seems so rational it is the opposite
don't for all that close reason's door
no one is waiting on the other side
only the eternal rich stealing from the eternal poor.

126.

Hard place to despair at morning
I know what I know and what good is that
self-knowledge is the same as self-delusion
lies you can use like homemade weather
the sun persists in rising romantic
call the world a cathedral and empty your pockets
call it a mosque and bow down
outside Eden the righteous anger of the uninformed
believe me there is only one conspiracy
the grammar of money burns a hole in your head
aftermath I said and molecule and touch your mother
too many people want nothing from me not.

127.

Light runs the machine
before sunrise no cloud no wind
and now the sky is full of tossing
no method only mind
consciousness is a habit of matter
it thinks where it can
that's where we come in
a freight train right through Callicoon
a little boy anxious about the sky
pine trees taller than anywhere
I came to life where Oedipus left it
every grove is sacred every girl a god.

128.

Not so limber when the light decides
you know all this is signs
a word on a truck goes by
you know I'm in love with you don't you
the hedge said it topiary of words
lost in the maze of a single straight line
does this street go to heaven
the word has no meaning in a world of streets
streetcorner the statues of Venus till the emperor wakes
between bed and bathroom the shadow of a dream
you don't know her name but that's all you don't know
steam locomotive, movie lovers in a lifeboat.

129.

To see anything at all is just remembering it
but the word you hear in silence is actually now
or five minutes of the future pulling you forward
a friend tugging you into the park
children sailing boats in the fountain woman eating corn
myriads mix the chessboard rises to the sky a rook topples
the tower falls towards you from an empty sky
it lands slowly and builds up around you
you have been spoken now
vague animals roam around the base in the dark
but at the top you still can see the sun
setting behind mountains that weren't there when you first looked.

130.

If the son knew the father as the mother knows the son
the gate would open and the world would enter in
Blake didn't say this but he meant it
children had no place in his world or mine except for me
eternal selfish child of self all brooding wanting
a child cancels the father and abandons the mother
that is how generations erase their past and are erased in turn
I am not prepared to say more than the words in your mouth
warm sun on chill morning no further than that
purple vestments today's mass mourning for last night
nothing special about her just that she was
washed by the wind instructed by her hair.

131.

Feelings are not to be reported feelings are to be felt
it's always winter again the mosaic of discourse starts up
where all the pieces fall asunder there is no answer
water table what the land will hold
turned away from the messaging sun the drenched moon
la Dranse flows north from glaciers fed
rain ratcheted can't tell who really means
all poems say the same thing don't you know that yet?
no time to mention a melon split open in the sun
what goes on in that dim town across the dream
roses on her thighs are blessed with thorns
I want to know who rings that bell and why.

132.

When is a wound like a wonder
miracle macula the kindly leper healed
by light alone inserted in the vascular
flesh-light cures all so little left
swimming up the arteries salmon-men
by contradiction reverse time's mindless flow
the opera is always just beginning
apotheosis of Ariadne creates heaven to be in
a place peopled only by who had been humans
now lift their syntax through the stars
radio blaring on the empty fishing boat
what music do they hear who empty out the sea?

133.

Heal like an open window an opus number a lost quartet
the sheen of shadow as if a word once spoken
the leaf speaks louder than the tree
the thing you need to know you never trust
Nietzsche, rose garden above Bolzano smell of asphalt
suicide because birds can walk but men can't fly
beautiful vow I vaunt that vaults to heaven
shield me from the hailstorm broken scraps of human will
because the will can live without its man
bring me unconsenting to my deed
a vow is medicine finally a use for pain
hawthorn berries to help my love's heart.

134.

We're still in opera that city where the music pays
intervals between the notes men do things to each other
a ring of rising thirds a single leap a ninth
girls turn into goddesses gods sweat to keep up with light
a handful of moon a head full of wheat
sleepy grain sleepy sunshine morning comes in vain
in sleep the words are hard to read
woman on the sofa what does she mean by sitting there
or the one on the floor reading the paper she is the news
touch the over-energy, *energumen* each one has
flows into other making both strong
it is the breath of the dæmon who lives our lives.

135.

No waiting it went and was now
all those old words that meant me stopped
as if the chalice never touched my lips or never left them
the weather is inside us too
knowing litters small birds along the sky
you are the architect of the obvious
things bow down at your feet you know me cold
morning was never meant for this to be obedient at last
hide your confession deep in your tract on ethics
explore the dream life of Immanuel Kant
exalt the triviality of poetry
where three roads meet the god is always present.

136.

Slow down a stoker in a locomotive old
Zola by Renoir Kafka's steamship balancing nowheres
can't help but making luminous mistakes
bathroom down the hall barefoot dawn
a room is just a footnote to its window
sun gleams on steel a pen seems muse enough
over the harbor slipping her sail so quiet beauty come
Azure as ever he teased the war over at last   LZ
now we can go home, home is always somewhere else
I watched my father shovel coal into the furnace
hand on the throttle of the door I made the house go
talked about coke but it was anthracite and Ellington.

137.

Door opening yoga frog croaking man lifting lumber
longer than I am this matter I uplift
subtended by substance the soul unveils
the Middle Ages never ended, the pilgrims saunter
all the kings of earth still fail their pentecosts
only the beauty is missing the flowing spontaneity of stone
Autun, we have our weathers too our smooth
flaming sunsets in suburban prose
will the sun on the sea be enough for me
sit on the ground and let the world tell
all your talk is reference book and parliament
what a body knows only your body can pronounce.

138.

A density of happening with no story to constrain it
don't look now we can't do anything anyhow
not all forlorn yet seigneurs we still are in Egypt
when we still had gods we still have names
reed dance where the Sawkill ponds out and beaver
things still live me a quiet world though I am not
mute magic an emperor ashamed to rule
all I ever want is the surfaces of things
the wicca of daylight on the night of things
Tristan on a rock no reason to be me
last night in shimmer I tried to count the sails
when you die you belong to everyone.

139.

Awn of oat and hawthorn berry
whose heart help they hear
for hearing is the same as healing
ads aver voices of the fishermen heal mute having
where owning is a silent tomb to be in
and the gull cries over the neighbor
but last night full moon in mist over Gayhead
the old light leaning through
here is a picture of you doing it
begin us again with the sky on your head
holy basil and petals from these very roses
who knew before now I owned the whole sea?

140.

Sleek to find you in a flutter of feeling
where the word fits among the mirror neurons
makes all the lovely errors wake up thinking
light comes off the quiet sea and hurts the eyes
hole in the middle of a word where breath comes in
the E of ear of seek of seen of Delphi
hope what the weather hopes and all will be
sparrows on the deck just watching them's a dance
did you know it was me before he told her
does even a child know what water does
patchwork sunlight through for once windless leaves
is it possible that light itself is sobbing and we hear?

141.

Mix the grains again for Psyche's pleasure
mess is comfort and the law-book torn
restore all the seeds to our original chaos
don't wander trying to set things straight
things are right to begin with, confusion is organic
this mess reminds me, Psyche yields to pleasure
always here and always now and always elegant
maiden gypsies tend their stallions' fetlocks
heel white runs right, heel dark can't walk
o fall over lightly Kentucky dreamer round heels
drink to soothe the seething a lie to cure the truth
so much sun today I can almost see.

142.

A word is as wide as the will and it's all for you
the hedger at his trim the blackbird mum
no sound but peopleness *menskr* all we bring
to the world is religion it does fine without
trying to find the way there he found a white lode
soft as clamshells of no use but to witches
his satin armband her linen garter bind
the meaty parts of going or of handling things
throb of artery renews appetite aloft
everything was right there the chemistry the harpsichord
some Chinese whispers from Ernst Toch she played me
the virgin queen with all my Tarot cards.

143.

Every work must be cosmology before biography
but the dinky little bits of life come in too
I tell you you are you and what can you contest
the lawn needs a shave it's Sunday and no bells
the mathematics of the wind *mathom* is treasure
rises when the sea heats up long after dawn
everything tends backwards witchcraft was no religion
we knew the things before we knew the knowers
now float rudderless paradise a lake not a garden
a well ensouled by circumstance
the ash we find after a stranger's bonfire on the beach
the old lost word that once meant god.

144.

Of course still worry about these things
the wind wants in, to read the words
wind carries in its lap, the seeds of sleep
mind in sleep renews its contract with the earth
the dance we call dream, that forgetting thing
there is no natural end to nature
hence all the busy carry up the hill
higher as if wiser so the sea forgets us
brass doorknob warm from the sun going in
how many times does a house get born
the sea's ceaseless baptism of the shore
and still we live in sin elves without a hill.

145.

One cloud in no sky
dying later sooner never
constant supervision of the real
humid means the air has breathed before
mean room in empty touristy hotel
only believe what wind tells in that other language
in brightest sunshine heard the child forgets
Ghost Trio playing to the sunset phrase
cart full of dead trees Atu XV everything changes
oxygen found on Mars iron on earth Blake in heaven
slowly adding and adding up to zero
the old couple next door suddenly look like kids.

146.

And ate this flower Old Man Is Young Again
I found it where the new snake left it
on cool cement by the house door agathodaimon
all the ceaseless gifts of living things
to those of us who soil the air with speaking
all our religions and dollar signs and sighs
and these sweet people gave us bass and fluke
to wind again the clock stopped when the old man died
the song they sadded me with when I was young
overwhelm me and be better each of us one step
use me all the way up
the strangest things can break the heart an empty room.

147.

Ariel pretends Prospero's his master
but no one rules that bright air eye
God's Lion strange name for a little bird
master of the island, human books flutter useless
no magic and no science stilts his liberty
to go and come and speak and ply his appetite
humans rough or gentle are his toys
he teases them by seeming to comply
catch wind in a handkerchief palace in your pocket
o I tried to rule those wizard wings one time
all I got was flutter and flap all my words dispersed
yet he brought me back my drownèd book again.

148.

Eden syndrome the better the place the more fear you'll be cast out
fundamental neurosis of the ecological moment
paranoid planet ruled by demons still
still we have to do something else about it
something abstract something works
footsteps down some distant wooden stairs
who comes to thrust us out we're not yet in
selves run out of self, a damp fog rolls in
bird feathers and no rain a song instead
meteoric solitude hurrying through emptiness
to be with you before you get to be
inconceivable meaningless such energies so-called stars.

149.

So as words vanish, they banish us from us
and some are singing as they leave the park
maybe a story is a wicked thing
tell what happened but not the happening?
better the man alone in a room
music comes somehow in
and nothing said or said not much
just let us look at a man all by himself
a woman sitting in her house alone
what kind of story could be better than silence
as if in Ovid a girl is changed into a girl
and there is no self to distract us with green leaves.

150.

No special moment for the clock to stop
o I'll get a headline out of that
you hear me better when you aren't listening
government a fancy word for the police
anybody knows what you mean but not what you say
saying is dark, dark, a tree lost in a forest
pluck this fruit and name yourself again
a nobody slipping under the giant's reach
Polyphemus is radar crouch to be unknown
miracle of neglect the oil of absence sweet
and so Blake seldom saw the sea and if he did
its size dissuaded him from the transports of love.

151.

Anchor lights the masts are gone now
blue collisions in this fog
a master of humility aquifer unsalt me
cleanse me of all matters till I am matter alone
much so much to ask an alchemist
chewing roses the taste is late to flower
then from every taste you're in the sudden garden
Gan Eden where the atmosphere stands guard
our other planet we are programmed to forget
each one of these must be at least a stone
how they look beneath an inch of clear water
how they look when you see me in her dream.

152.

Time a shadow cast by heavenly event
name me in your sleep
for when I sleep it is a fierce and silent place
I don't know how to touch you there
and then the birds are slow to sing at dawn
birth cry of a lone old man hoarse mourning dove
I move my head the face in the mirror doesn't move
at night she can't escape the color of her dress
it makes the sun keep rising everywhere she goes
I dare you not to look at me I am a mirror
I wear glass wherever I go no wonder you're silent
not even the rain has so much to say.

153.

A man's voice and a woman's voice at once
I have to check these clues with my therapist
my vow stands beside me and saves me from myself
leave your letter in plain sight to baffle the police
bird further away the hill to hear us
one day I swear it they'll come out from the hills again
cleanse us of this debt-crazed world
whip the money-makers out of this temple world
how dare you listen to music doesn't it tell you something
fragments of silence all we need is a window
to believe we are the only ones is blasphemy
listen to those who walk invisible and talk to them too.

154.

Quiet describing landscape never seen
by names alone a wind comes through the fog
a wave moves through the sea displacing nothing
matter is not the same as what it does
there is a mindful moving in all things
but talk about love instead, the cellist's bare knees
press the earphone closer to the silence
wanted to sit all day and think but not think thoughts
just the ordinary mistral just the light passing by
impossible angles the edges of lost things
they scare me more than a half-eaten apple
Eve's disobedience still not quite complete.

155.

This still is Eden but who'll believe me
I meant only to complain lawnmowers erased the cello solo
but then the sun suffused the fog and no one listened
to anything but the noise that silenced me
this still is Eden some of us never left
a flaming sword that keeps you out lights us to our beds
because we sleep in matter
mind has burned away all its guesses
too much weight groan of a physical world
the wind in Eden my mother crying
or a story she could understand when I had come
beyond all stories to the untellable itself.

156.

One of those days when all music sounds like church
the wind is up to something
breath tries to remind us to let go
it has no natural end no golden fleece
only the dragon car on the merry-go-round
I rode it pompous to ride with Medea
the invisible beings who guide and protect
y ddraig goch for instance small monster in my blood
enough of Being it's time for the Is
the self-existent the shadow of a woman the mother's dream
Amphitrite comes before all and Ovid names her first
goddess of the ocean from whom we come and we are hers.

157.

Asprawl on lawn in pose of Titian's Danaë in exiguous bikini
she welcomed the island weather the sun knew her deep
and I looked away at all the other pictures on the air
every mistake needs its own footnote
everything means he said again
if Offenbach can be a Jew then I can too
the gondola took all my doubts away
I too heard the dead contralto singing from the wall
and all my tragic love affairs are comedies
the Muse told me stick to the skin you know
the giddy surfaces of human life, skip the abyss
forget silly Scamander where silly heroes fight and die.

158.

Only in the heart the blue flower grows, tells the one who finds it
climb into your body and drive to the other side of truth
someone is waiting there and always for you
the sentimental abstract blood trickles sweet bite
grasses on the high moors unanimous in wind
nothing can live at this altitude a steeple
I want to be at home as things are
but that's a kind of cardboard Africa
live where no one ever imagined
is that the famous blue flower
or the White Rose of national decency
for which the young students suffered and died?

159.

Binary as if a double star you are
two houses and two voices to proclaim
absolute and relative are the same
two doors to every thought like Boston flats
the law makes difference the will makes same
watch the sun rise little by little the light says yes
the wind is always coming from the night
the dark breathes for us
lost in childhood with a single book
greatness means to have no private life
sun up now and here the great one comes
all work is play at best.

160.

Ate roses from the rocks along the shore
one day she'll come walking over the sea
to restore us to our original forms
we mild impersonators of another story
cantilena of the obvious above the Hidden Theme
pick the ocean up and do what with it
one crow before anybody
I don't send news to the tailor how I wear my clothes
but I tell every sailor where to steer his craft
helmsman of absence monsignor of milk
scared except to be at home and there too
we have come to the midpoint of time.

161.

I had a dream you told me you had a dream about me
part of me on the other hand already is a dream
how many do I have to be to be one
it is a question of what kind of blue a flower
what kind of kind
when there was nothing but sea there still was me
I am plenty of you
an unfamiliar bird just now Berlioz must have been like that
little histories of what never happened
nation A beats nation B but war beats both of them
who are you crying to on your hilltop
the wind knows how to take your breath away.

162.

Far pillboxes over the heel of her island
sideways to wind sucks my breath away
all the familiars sieve through the mind
into the dark of other people's memories
what I lose you find a carousel of naughty children
seacoast is never far from mind it is made of it
ocean our first brain
resemblance is a wilted flower
no one told me anything but you
the stone that sealed him in he carries in his hand
every funeral seems to be my own
all religions are none I thought he said.

163.

Hard to read the numbers in this light
go by the feel of the machine, road through water
voices in the street fear of believing
whatever they say must be wrong way round
nobody out there speaks our language
urgent children touching in the dark
who are those who move around inside me
she walks by with a woodpecker on her back
to prove that language is a function of the skin
because language is all boundary
a walled garden and a maze at the middle
and a mirror globe at the center with roses all round it.

164.

Collecting stamps and never sending mail
nobody writes letters anymore
people are afraid of words in the hand
let Bach tell me six times what to do next
translate into something we can keep inside
inside us or in our household god *domovoi*
Lisa's plump white arms in Ivan's dying brain
we have to know though where everything belongs
o Egypt I am weak the rolled-up carpet weighs too much
all the streets led up to the castle where no one lives
you have to keep it all inside *la musique*
and when the morning finally comes the string will break.

165.

Or morning only comes when something breaks
how to tell your mother you're gay
the stains your pleasures leave on you
the roof cracks the birds fly out
it was no house after all it was the woods
only halfway through the catalogue of sins
remember never to confess unless confessing is a pleasure too
girl fell off the lighthouse made her lover fall
both drowned our coasts unguarded
deep-rooted on a shelf of rock below the sea
some sins will never wash away
one slight twist it comes off in your hand.

166.

A wave is pure motion in substance with no substance of its own
a brilliant shadow of a man at sea
left in a terra cotta lekythos takes two to hold it up
ten to drink it dry not ten of our kind ten of theirs
let Ovid tell the story his own way forget the Greeks
they are not in your blood your bloody veil
Mavors inside me made me leap three times
over the solstice fire into the sea of Seven Oxen
I swam to Venus though I cannot swim
walked gingerly on my friend's adventure
at the intersection of now and then a yellow flag
come not aboard this plague ship of love's sicknesses.

167.

Open the door and let your neighbor out
always somewhere waiting to be else
you know your dove by how the tail is shaped
what will heather do when weather changes
or rabbit in high grass or the four rivers of Kailasa
where the wing begins to wonder the chicks fly
thus go I clutching to the shoulders of the world
around me wrack of history walk on clean feet
feeding ourselves on what no man knows and all women do
each *polis* had its cult and we have none
the Reformation broke all that away
and *nation* made nonsense of what was left.

168.

Be suspicious of Greek models we are not Greeks
have no polis have no common practice to the gods
education is sick with Hellenic fundamentalism
Greek can be as bad as Bible for the soul
yet the poetry of both perdures illuminates
Dante is close because each walks the woods alone
the matter world of things receding
tailor sitting on his table stitching what we all must wear
the technology of magic haunts us now
to walk invisible in Google goggles isolate
how soon Ariel goes into Caliban
when once before the magus left the island to the sea.

169.

I think I counted wrong I'm not the only one
there is a wolf beside me and a kingbird in the tree
beast and bird and me can't know as much as one woman can
call us all to bed and see what happens then
the Irish poets worked for pay the pay was praise
fat salmon in the cooking pot poetry is war without an enemy
when 'faith' replaces cult the *polis* is dead
the Greeks never had to believe anything they knew, they did
as Jung at the end said "I don't have to believe, I know"   *CGJ*
faith cuts us apart from one another
believe nothing and do everything, and conversely
both ways make wise, help the wind blow.

170.

I'm never shy of naming elements
the things that were here for us before we knew
so those are the colors of my spectrum
those are the blocks I fiddle with
rousing to you impatient to stroll
road in shadow past a donkey in a field
a hill up ahead but everyone speaks French
and none of this was here before the ground
so I will go to my mothers below the hill
and live among the ferly folk as though I were a man
and listen to their practice of sun and moon
and learn enough to come back in a hundred years and all for you.

171.

Rescuing forever from never I put the writing in your hand
come back from the place that never was
when the city deserts its gods flee to the fields
in woods gods won't leave you alone, you pray by breathing
and even so you have to write it down
this is your sole commandment listen and repeat
because the word you hear changes in you to the word you say
and only you can say it world without end amen
but the Mass your body is is always beginning
your body is praying all the times
knows more about the gods than Socrates
if you don't know the answer no one does.

172.

Be careful of numbers that come into your head
light-filled windows of an empty house
listening is filling a jug with water from a slow fountain
listening is walking down a street you never saw
walk the grass between the sidewalk and the curb
to be in the between is to be born again
any tween space is the primal cave
the folk you see around you are bisons on the wall
every salesman a high priest, grammar a wizard's spell
the witches love you and the birds are all machines
you wind up the engine with your first breath
keep breathing or all the lights go out.

173.

The rule is so simple make people happy
the method is harder live for the other
the gods come only when they're needed
as that girl he thought he knew once
came along and guided Dante to the rose
but was she the same as the one who knew
or never knew, you can't tell by looking
but the telling does no good till you tell it
the breath you breathe out different from what you breathe in
measure the difference in a world full of commas
listen long enough and learn to tell lies
don't stand by your words walk behind them find the way home.

174.

He's getting smart it must be near the end
he has no clue to what the house is called
why does a castle need a name it has a moat
all we need is difference did he say
all belief is make-believe
deus adest alteri drink from the well
the healing breath of other people no help in same
stay far enough away so that they still are other
the mess of mingling knows no edge
boundary is all, we're bound to mark
mark we honor by transgressing
travel far by staying home.

175.

Everything over the sheen belongs to me
schön shiny things are fair to be
privilege of silver your own moon in the sky
a body lingers telling time away from me
the belt of storms marks out the parallax of lust
is it you or is it me stand witness for the light
hydrogen and helium burn to make us see
or is there a light that comes before the sun
come and come again disorder ferries me to you
through the window a warrior dying on the beach
once we were Vikings now we are stones
the oldest dream you ever had becomes your life.

176.

Some texts only dare to read by day
David's harp strings cut for the sake of the song
how should an old man dance before the Ark
to what old music Biber Schubert Karamanov
body's an embarrassment in church
folly to the Greeks dance with your tongue
till the song goes to sleep along the spine
why does sun on the sea smell like toast
the word remember is like roasted meat
when there is nothing left but to recall
call again and hope they hear you but who
when you meant me what name did you actually say?

177.

Tongue the flute lower there is a deeper music
indefatigably mental a fiddle golf cart in Judæa
all I have are Promised Lands
spent this life writing down the wind
spread on the lawn to welcome godly showers
hear the copter see only how white clouds roar
indecisive moment the taste of glass
the great gate of Kiyiv never opens never closes
a gate is a man standing in the desert
Stonehenge is a ring of girls around a message
they said a storm is coming love gets lost in theory
revolutions are ninety-nine percent revenge.

178.

Swimming in rain the lightning swims with you
we still don't know what it is this electric thing
hydrangeas struck by lightning reading Montaigne in the park
one fugue for a thousand voices
ghosts at midday the darkest time of soul
wait for the re-entrance of the theme: the bay of Naples
dark as I am don't confuse me with the dark
look at the sea through a man with an old straw hat
the sea you say is not the same sea
or we were tortured by our differences
I've been seeing ghosts all day
a ghost is a man without a man.

179.

Penny rolling down an inclined plane
or planet on its roll around a flaming doubt
I knew you when you were my mind before
no one took but everybody takes
cleared a forest to liberate the moon
beautiful astronomy before numbers were invented
one day there was nothing left to count
could you catch it from the bite of an idea
there are no comparisons or only one
paper doesn't drink up the way it used to
one mind shadows another
wake up some morning and think with me.

180.

Trace the themes that wind the fugue
deep undergrowth this year in aspen grove
all lines lead back onto your hand
line of fate line of wheat
how many kids all the disasters of love
scribbled on the palm grey clouds coming
woodland cabin of the arbiter of dreams
where the bishop of permissions was conceived
it's all a merry-go-round some horses go up and down
some horses just as beautiful understand to stand still
harnessed in pretty glass rubies of samsara
all the love you give comes back to you.

181.

Infant voices shrill to cry for help
soaked by Niagara to understand Canadian
the doctor complained I failed to signal pain
fall deepest in love with whatever you don't know
release the sky from labor let the lighthouse do it
something to steer by only one horse on the island
this glass of water that I prove to you
ran through all the rivers of the world to get to you
every word is an exaggeration
I saw a trickle of wine on the Savior's chin
I waited and everything revealed just keep talking
those who saw her knew enough to look away.

182.

There is another story I'm not allowed to know
I'm reading one book the story's in another all the time
the Empty Story I need above all deeds
the normal lights the way to the story of any story
the skeleton who sings the ribcage knows how to think
o neurons mother of my little world
Hölderlin's roses bloomed last month some still linger
these gulls seem to be asleep as they fly
like swallows above Lacoste who sleep all night midair
where Mary of Magdala saw them first and cried
so that her Husband looked up too and spoke
everyone will rise again and none fall back.

183.

In the garden of the undecided
raptors quick in surf to dive a cormorant
quarrying the sea
the end of matter is an ardent remember
words change their clothes for winter
a fugue is never far
it is an honest man who says such things
refuted by the first green tide
merciful fog hiding colors in plain sight
once a lost battalion stumbled on a black lake
thousands of cranes in a pearly mist
and knew they had come home.

184.

All the lands of never waiting for me
wonder why the ink itself won't sing
all words belong to someone else
borrow this gypsy hen her magic egg
praise is vital though it turns to ash before the shrine
spice of incense burning down
solve all my problems easy as say no
signpost at the crossroads between Neaux and Hiesse
strong sun in cucumber slice open midnight
that's how the stars began mind started counting
I need a maid to pick up all these stones
a world swept clean of what I mean.

185.

All these animals waiting for me
a tiler waiting for a wall mosaic Christian floor
I once knew how to walk that street
I see a word I never touched before
raindrops impersonate pale flowers
all these headlines try to hold your mind
hint at what each sentence means to reveal
verbs confuse sentences as sudden movements startle birds
the nouns you almost trust as if the Middle Ages
came round to you again and all your shirts
smelled of lavender and any maiden with a lute
could drive you crazy with likely continuities.

186.

Now there was a man the ferly folk took away
they brought him to a time between times and loved him there
left a lookalike back home to do his job
while he did theirs and the work they had to do
is all praising and delighting in them
for they were born before the world and wonder still
what manner people we are who hardly know them
let alone praise their sacred everlasting beauty
so he lived with them in some blessed island
till he understood at last what pleasure is
and shared it with the little brooks and the trees
and the ferly folk marveled at his industry.

187.

Lie here because there is nowhere else ever
the word gave birth to me and I may have failed the word
friend's face among the flowers smiling up
the image does not please me you never can
tell what a smile is smiling at
animal wisdom I need you near
only a beast knows when to turn away
a man by the nature of time will walk to the abyss
Empedocles Master of Consequences to vanish in thin air
hum hum hymn of the volcano
a story broken in half we hold the stub
the other part of it or anything blows away.

188.

The breeze stops when I open my eyes
someone is watching me powerful and far
I close my eyes again and doze into blue
and then I am away with everything else
we live remote and love alike
sky white sea green we imagine difference and live with it
wave travels into mist makes island seem
name it and storm ashore
this is my kingdom of a moment
eternity a puff of breeze
if I try to walk there I will never come back
I never come back.

189.

He will be safer as a ferly-man if men they have or are
he will be a leper-man in ordinary land
his voice the bell to warn away the fearful
because language is a holy terror believe me
hide yourself in the silence of story
there's always something left to believe
dust for sparrows said the old aesthete
be bathed clean in what defiles us
Arbeit, heilende Welle in what defines us   *FB*
how far inland we've been carried by the wave
left where no other wave can come
lost among friends in a house of one's own.

190.

Poet heers a worke beseeming you   *CM*
not war but warbling kiss the girls and make them cry
all the holy raptures of the local mind
when I wanted clarion Gabriel renew the world
now blow your horn and if you can
shock the morbid loves into new play *lila*
mother of the mind the play of light all over
the light was like a woman in the trees man on a rock
and in our little ears the mountain spoke
a fleet of do's and don't's assail the lucid now
I am the hole in your pocket
your hand can't leave me alone.

191.

So much denial kings before Eden
nothing was ever, all the rest was obvious
Orpheus exiting from the underside of words
can only tell the mind that comes to speak
but o no o no the music always wins
flee back to ferly land and talk to daisies
feast on clover and try to be
superbly be, as if a lion walked off a coat of arms
and moved into one turret on my tower
and we lived together beside an almond tree
the weather always told us what to do
look over the wheat field a ship comes sailing.

192.

And there are the children at the gate
the psalmists keening by the hilltop shrines
the lean poesy of denunciation
when praise is all the air that feeds
go where every leaf has a word on it
our holy fire once for all
it spoke and said Do not be all male
for the masculine alone is weak
terribly weak and needy of conflict to assert
what cannot be asserted
the unprovable axiom of manhood
building empires wrong again and again wind blows away.

193.

The stones begin to speak now
tell me all I know
long ago but all too close the trees
whose house is that with one light showing
I dug a well where no water was
I built a staircase down to solid rock
no root cellar no smell of winter apples
spread the table with no cloth
on each empty plate a spoon of dust
don't waste the fuel of breath on flames
sit quiet with the shivered memories of your life
now you can do nothing but listen and no one speaks.

194.

The poor poor blame the billionaires
who all say the poor are to blame
so many of them! wanting to have more more—
isn't there a way of wanting less
no food no shelter no want at all?
But if all the poor laughed all at once
the billionaires would crumple up and blow away
he said so just be hungry with a smile
be lonely and speak to no one
already the ink on dollar bills is fading
already the water in your well turns into wine
already gold melts, pours out a highway to some world.

195.

Posthuman is to be beyond desire
to want no more than wood does
standing in the sunlight in the snow
making more of us by being so
and those stones know us too
one day calcium will have a voice
garnet in the Adirondacks speak
red wisdom to the risen poor
be enough the other side to be!
this is politics the throb of music
Bartok Beethoven Bruckner Bach.

196.

How heavy the weight of blank paper
carried all my life, in blunt photography
spiritual effluent of Eusapia Palladino
the crux of psychic plausibility
does all this light come out of one woman's body
is there any other source for splendor in the world
om tare tutare ture soha
she is sixteen still green in the ways of men
and she alone can save us from calamity
or tell us who can
listen to the green girl at last
the ever-virgin the truth the wisdom sleeps beside me.

197.

As if in mime an elegant body told
the whole story from grassland to cathedral
innumerable declensions of her single noun
the dancer absolute
so the mild persistent taste of moving anywhere
from lawn to grass again the poor smell of money too
we live in poverty we shadows of some great wealth
the potentates whose kingdoms fit in their wallets
they rule the world but we could too
as this lone dancer springs up from the sounding floor
and with a single swerve of movement
changes space forever in the way we see.

198.

The only thing that can't go on is going on
every perceptual quantum begins it all again
only the qualia sometimes linger
poor Abelard *o quanta qualia*
the golden sabbaths of the wounded heart
wanting to know how to make it go
don't let the children come in
all birds belong to you and fish are mine
pale wild-eyed ones swimming in my cavern
we who walk along the ground the strangest are
misshapen by desire bent over a bad book
our whole lives pictured there in code.

199.

Muybridge photos of a breaking heart
a daffodil in haste a monkey in a window
a dreary paper they call The Daily Olds
deer are watching from the new-grown woods
how many years have they been here
looking, crashing into cars, waiting for something
waiting for us to do something about ourselves
units of intelligent remorse
all the broken answers
war is never an option war is never
bring me your hand to hold at least
the old man's sword used to cut bread.

200.

Don't put up more signs
I hear them hammer their stakes in
for sale signs by frightened houses
how poignant to move among the living
how her body leaps to welcome 'circumstance'
what the editor wrote down instead of 'God'
haunted by temple friezes a harlot in heaven
noble souls entrusted to my care
catch a reflection of the rising sun
outline with pencil the shadows of the leaves   *RH*
till all the trees are written down
then sleep beside it till the rooster crows.

201.

I hear him over the hill or is that the sun in my eyes
a picture long enough to wrap around your waist
and go romancing in an old book
slippery pavement on the road to Neaux
in this cicada year the moon says less
moon no bigger than a mosquito
moon buzzing in my eyes
till the cock crowed and here I am
cicadas fuguing with the buzz-buzz in my ears
with one hypnotic pass I wake me up
look Robert there are days inside the day
the birds are gone but the sky is still there.

202.

Could I have heard another when I thought was now
leave every I out and see what it means
real presence split the log he is there
drink salvation from an empty glass
too many voices for so few words
we suffer from the vice of versa
they marched to battle with The World Turned Upside Down
revolution only benefits the landlords old or new
would she kiss the icon of a commissar?
at some point or no point it will get tired of me
then what will you do
not even the wind in your ears?

203.

Starting and stopping is the same as love
properties of archaic Tocharian
guide me grammar through the spiel of trees
obscure selvedge of a vast weave
a carpet made of sand
flowers half faded dinky here and there
your footsteps rearrange the floor
walking and talking like a blessed Greek
they didn't know how lucky they were
pagans are the only ones left laughing
after the grimoire of the bank accounts
the Grand Guignol of local government.

204.

Maddening stillness of the summer air
here as if nobody's there, nobody cares
I come from wind and you far more
crystal movement of the invisible
emphasis belongs to humankind
gods write the book we put the italics in
the trouble is as with Hopkins' beauty
it never seems not to be a poem
never a simple language thing that happens by
still seizes the breath or chills the heart
there has to be nobody listening when I speak
so that the words break free to all of you.

205.

Now of the cicadas from their long sleep
awoke and bred and did and sang and now to bed again
what are we to some glorious animal
eloquent in hyperspace our spit their silver
because we make much of things
art is Latin for the way of making
the way of making is so our only way
childish wits suppose we too were made
no god ever had the art of us
we came out of the sea and from the ground
we mated in bold daylight and we did
and we do.

206.

If a thing can be itself and still go on
that is the raw meat in the rhapsode's song
people all over pretending to be me
clear as Chesterton in the gloaming of the evening
would I were my father's favorite word
not twitch so while I'm saying so
I can hardly read the word I write why I need you
there are spirits here antagonists of air
is it prayer that sifts all round us and we breathe in
what one word be scents the garden of Adonis
sacrifice means taboo only gods can have it
what would the world be like if we were in it.

207.

Every question is a trick
do you think no I only quote
comparisons are bad for the environment
don't sit next to me while you're quoting
I never want to hear what wise men said
do you think I want to walk out in someone else's clothes
don't make such a fuss just forget about it
forgetting is the hardest thing of all
that's why you fled your island isn't it
why you sailed up the dark river not even the trees knew you
that's why you write down what other people say
you make them up to talk to you so somebody remembers.

208.

Forgive that little *lude* or play between the going on
I lost the knack of not answering myself
I stand accused of lying down a folly to the Greeks
of rising up again at cock-crow and my people know me not
for I was married to a windmill and a lake
in summer rain every green a different color
I set it down meaning to revere it later
then came Cossack horsemen through the shtetl of my brain
and who knows now where reverence went
thirteen Jews at a table telling the joke that is God
who when he was lifted up healed all the world but not himself
sunrise from the earth he had no self to heal.

209.

I'm still with Abbot Benedict still with Malory
cannonshot was supposed to be the end of us
the middle time we called it when we were young in it
now it's only now and Internet our Maimonides
everything lasts everything changes no one remembers
pleasure is the only gift study how to please
lasts as long as Christmas seventeen years and come again
I want to know the cycle of each thing
lifespan of the chickadee of Niagara
of me for that matter but nobody knows
how well we'd live if we knew the date of our demise
olé! I die today.

210.

So pleasure it is, pleasure and praise
the rain has stopped the colors last
don't look back it's only a flower gaining on you
only a womb anxious to reclaim me
last night on the island I saw exact in dark my mother's face
let me learn to say this countenance
expressionless veridical completely there
to be fully seen is to be present
have I lived up to anything she proposed
we don't know what we ask of one another
what we give we hope is what was wanted
such gifts are absolute no giver no receiver.

211.

Solitude, light rain, kindness kiss the sweat off his back
let him go the world's big enough
to be big enough for the smallest words
argent, a tower gules and then he said
from this window she can see anyone who comes and goes
but everyone is upside-down
man coughing in the morning breeze
how does she keep all that she sees from floating away
to build a thing and then believe in it
a tower or a testament
Dostoyevsky railed against mere chemistry
the bonds that love us into one another's lives.

212.

This is Book VIII of the Aeneid
we finally go inland here
where the dark river loves us
into the unknown interior of your house
where maples hang over slow waters
when we look down to see our faces we see nothing
the water has faces of its own
animals (this is all about animals) begin to talk now
we write home saying "animals talk to us now
what are we going to do with our silences
our precious silence?" but no letters come back
deer run right into us we can't understand the crows.

213.

I thought she was grieving in her ogival cloak
her face white but when I bent to console her
she was laughing she comforted me
she put words in my mouth I wake half-healed
have to live this clear thing not just know it
her word was sweet and I spoke it all day
in the dark country where everybody lives
keening sometimes or laughing at the faces
peering out from the hillside ancient still young
their skin soft as lamb's ears pale as mistletoe
they look as if they remember me
but who am I now?

214.

Sometimes finish something enough to begin with
'a balanced aquarium'
Antin explained when we were kids
so much I learned from him I'll never admit
plants feed fish excrete feed plants
oxygen out of nowhere
only the sun needs helium
at the other end of its cosmos last dream's gentlest touch
thrill the way a bird does or morning light
mockingbird on the bridge in rain
where herons often glide from pond to bay
I'm gasping for breath airless in Gaza
to see me suffer puts the leaves to sleep.

215.

Night stuff thick
ankles of consciousness
slow drag a thickened broth
a cake of beef fat offered to birds
there are days music will not listen
means that no one hears
after a month on the sea it is hard to be anybody else
say it with your hands the way the night
is religion only something other people do
glamor of the ivory corpus constantly reminds
once there was a place where these things mean
thank God we have to make our own.

216.

Walk over there and meet myself departing
signs of death I cannot find my shoes
lost my heart in the Rockaways
began to think that love was made of skin
cathedrals walk beside you when you go
I flew over the Hadramawt and Mars looked back
the meaningless politeness of the desert rock
the empty cup I offer to my friends
how little I've given, how much proposed
littoral birds the afikomen found at last
set me my place at the table near the door
sometimes the sight of food makes me despair.

217.

To measure a day by a meaning
lean crystals sift into your lap
the varieties of greens exhaust vocabulary
no need to describe what everyone remembers
the whole street a secret garden a hidden sign
even a name knows how to hold your hand
wise fingers apportion peace and war
but have I forgiven all those I hurt
shutters up on the primeval coast
we help each other wade ashore
and nothing more
the gift just happens the sun just rose.

218.

Do it the easy way begin with someone else
we dance in trance a rhetoric of selfishness
all we have to give our bodies are
we choose our functions in a balanced world
whatever it is it always works
that's the mind for you
no escape from the balanced aquarium
we live and die as suits another and we are that other
so relax and try to cheat less on your taxes
it doesn't work it all comes out of you
can't save can't spend can't mar can't mend
free will is an advertising ploy.

219.

You are the debt that has to be repaid
your habit patterns are your only cage
stay far away from wanting more
more humility among the trees
the cicadas have done their work and gone
leaving each Egyptian carapace behind
our window screen and blacktop and the lawn
worn out from sheer song fallen
Babylonian with black and gold
I am your mother too don't you remember
London Bridge and looked upstream
into the far west we come from now.

220.

Call it weather it will watch you bird-eyed with wary
you came to rape our fields and steal our sheep
nothing we can do to stop you but it can
it knows the way you Troyans trust in signs
the white pig nestled in leaf shadow
the cloud walking girl-like up the oak-weary hill
we will give you more signs than you can read
you'll never trust your bed again with all our dreams
this is our land and we are semaphores
we can't do anything but fill your senses
every sense complete and all the information false
only the truth can really lead you wrong.

221.

I never knew anything it was all made up
all bluff and prophecy
willful history of our feigned race
imaginary archive of testicular witness
none of the cathedrals were real
none of the bridges skating rinks nudist beaches
stockmarkets rainstorms Glastonbury
all loving lies I made for you
all Plotinus all Shakespeare Nag Hammadi
the lotus garden where the princess yawned
brass basins of the Temple the rights of man
national debt all lies and all for you.

222.

Perception of the other is the first mistake
till then Mind is peace and luminous
once it senses other all the stuff begins
the offerings and arsenal the blood and fear
until the only cure for me is to be you
make the glad of the other my whole work
then mind will be mine again
full of its own serene excitements
beyond the dark and light
try it if you don't believe me
do enough for the other and nothing for me
let the ocean show the quick way home.

223.

Then again the linden trees this year blossomed
we sleep and wake in the scent of them
pale obscure little flowers that fill the night air
but am I a character in your epic
uneasy narrative of words spewing words
stochastic craziness full of ancient Greek
when I just want to smell the flowers
rest again on someone's cheek
as if the war had never shattered my electron shell
left me gasping naked on the shingle beach
before the monsters crept back to the deep
and the ospreys dropped fish for me to eat.

224.

Long comber by the shore of ease
why did we ever leave
who are you talking to now
in red or in bed
the harsh bondage of rhyme
subtle bondage of sound
by *klang* alone bring matter in   JT
will heal the legend lost souls of this pale day
find me kindling for my water
dig a hole in air and shove me in
the sound of a word is a niche around me
sense turns me marble from head to toe.

225.

Born again normal in a nullish world
dance in the drugstore waiting for your pills
description *is* prescription
ask the subway florist for gardenia
you'll see why later she explained
walk along the esplanade all those ships are thee
nothing's better left unsaid
or are you Irish before all and grassy
I want to know where the lost ones live
touching our fingertips together is enough to start the dance
a flaw in the pattern is the meaning of the weave
a gnat drinking salt from a child's eye.

226.

Music finds you
it was made to do that
to be small and slip in everywhere
the crawl of beauty through the null
you don't hear anything if you listen
don't listen to the quartet like a mechanic checking the engine
listen to music the way you go to sleep all of you at once
anything else is college stuff
required courses in tonality reality
a proud humility is the way to do anything
listen reverent as a king hearing the first robin in spring
can you do that can you take it gently in the hands of your ears.

227.

Of course do it for the other the hot blue sky
what hurts us helps the corn
protein the decisive factor in cultural history
egg white is intellect tempera and madrigal
for I was another country when I slept
and now am you
Interdependence Day each man a king
belonging to one another we are spoken from Being
he was the only one who made some sense and look what happened
marauding mind trapped in a stale idea it had
horror of hurting another for the sake of an idea
Bruno burnt among flowers.

228.

You don't need me to tell it is never right to kill
Holocaust or unsolved murder
only the numbers are different
to kill one person is to kill the world
capital punishment corrodes the state
to kill one woman destroys the human race
Jesus was a man murdered by the state
that's all you need to know about the government
no one ever has the right to kill
this is the only thing I know
and out of it I lift stone by stone my feeble tower
to make a work where all of you are safe.

229.

But from its top I can behold the sea
across the street our little stream in spate she said
ironies and departures
you know how to get here start from here
a little movement in the leaves says I'm alive
everything I give you is a sign
this is the blank sign
carry it with you till rain or sun
shadows the blankness with messages
then think they come from me
who have nothing else to give you
just one word after the last word.

230.

Pause in the middle of meaning and mean something else
there is no road or rule just tree-frogs singing
just blue sky gleaming through dense green leaves
everything is an interruption
the newborn innocent screaming
a day red in the face angry at wordless men
they try their ruler games but weather is god
I'm not saying I'm just saying
if this is not me talking then who are you
from the torn purse no gold coins spill
long low quiet run of Avenue R
civilization is built on personal discomfort.

231.

When I said enough you weren't listening
a phone rings far away and only there
why do we care about the colors aren't they the whole story
all the colors of Tara the single blue of the Medicine Buddha
look around you'll see them everywhere
on different instruments how can one note be the same
or there is no such as same
when the mind is busy we are no years old
night and morning fragrant linden flowers fade now
lindens and cicadas and sunspots who else is there
tiny homeopathic breeze to make the skin joy
color is the other word for it.

232.

Does it even sound like this
is it music or does it mean
he asked an anger layer of low cloud
but there was only blue and shapeliness was you
there is no plausible verb for being
too many people were far away and didn't care
the pink and tinseled rider in the circus
who knows from where such people come
if people they are if come they do
I started watching as a child and never stopped
in the barnyard with ruddy feathers
the names of creatures are the same as sleep.

233.

Measure not pleasure
the ripest ambiguity high priestess
golden color quiet lioness
heel heel great varmint of the sky
soon it will be your turn, wheel
can I ever other? Bruno argued yes
I rage at how they fired him
restoring him to his elements
yes change your horoscope revise the sky
the people waiting for you are hiding in your sleep
take the iron road that ran right in
crying his name she came to herself alone.

234.

And that was how she was a Tarot card
naked visible through a brick wall
a window where none was possible
she made the light and he brought the air
the wind was seeing her with his pale eyes
she breathed in being seen and so we move
to the next gallery every image is a room of its own
come live me inside the image
the deeper in you go the more space there is
we come through a small door into a big world
in this way we enter every image
hold the image in your mouth and taste the remember.

235.

Of engine what to speak how things are made to happen
Persephone herself bent to retrieve
sky color from earth color
our first ethnographer she is taken
taken in by what she investigates
and lords it later over the dead and not yet born
Hades' house is not just for the dead
it is the queendom of everything unseen
she ladies it over hell where we all are fat
swollen with pasts and lives to come
all for the sake of one blue flower and no mother
she is her own mother now.

236.

Now light your heart and be another
time is weary of this mask of yours
melt the wax of it away in seventh-month heat
be free of this prison thee
I am little but mythological chatter
break the light a little and come home
nothing happens on the other side
until we wake again with human faces
I look more like you than you believe
finally divided sunlight into heat like a message
someone sends you find some shade and stand there
there is a Golem in all of us a servant heavy slumbering.

ɣ

237.

But I can only be the same as me a little while
Gettysburg grandfathers battle scars
isn't it enough that we still are
begin by blaming money the opposite of language
blame mathematics and greed and value
then blame the summer stars for being many
anxious sperm that quest the eggs of mind
always trying to mean something in me
blame mastery and alpha and volcano
the love that hurtles through the woods of Ireland
the ones that we cut down to reach the sea
but never blame the sea.

238.

Revise my chapel of this local stone
build the sky into the window
let it have edges but no walls
change the images of gods displayed
change the gods
fill the pews with water
no prayer on dry land makes sense
stand up to your waist in wave recite the alphabet
alphabet with variations
this is your liturgy your people you
I am the altar but don't look at me
taste the water now then listen to what you say.

239.

You knew theology had to come of this
what else is interesting but to speak of gods
translate sex into language yields theology
(discourse on the knowable written with mind on something else)
poetry at least is always about itself
but the poem has no self it is pure act
hence more or less useful to everybody like light
even in the dark you think about times you saw
and if I die before I wake
drive a red car to my funeral
do Beethoven with blue flowers
call me by your own names as you mourn.

240.

But each of these is many more than one
time to talk big so I seem small
radishes from a lover's garden
dense symbolism of the subway
Muscovite manners how soon they forget
I'm not complaining I'm admiring
a Renoir walking out of the loo
a cynical note a poke at Uncle Toby
I had no war of my own
my mental strife was all with me
I despair of the city he said
the city did this to me.

241.

And so gave up Jerusalem
want the trees before the clearing
no temple's worth a living tree
let alone fifty acres of English oak
culled to craft one warship then
days you could still see the goddess in the trees
before the parsons bored all life away
in windowless cenacles clustered round guilt
grrrr I will wolf this land anew and lie on it
I thought you said you had no enemies
no I have no war my enemies are friends
I do what you tell me who else is there.

242.

A lyric absence though birds mute trees
lyric means doing something to the air
lyric means the right to be wrong
keep company with dumb ideas
sailing paper metaphors around the room
lyric means knocking on a wall and crying Open
lyric means being baffled by an open door
lyric love is not like other kinds
flowers bought in the supermarket
the old mast of the *Ernestina* lying on the dock
heartwood still fresh after a hundred years
lyric means the heartwood of a living tree.

243.

All the definitions are now in place
revise the animal feed it from your lap
a bee knows by
the is the center of the maze
woodpecker gospelling a dead tree
bird bath tepid on the lawn
be quiet we are someone here
try to be as quiet as it is
we are not meant to live together
each human is alone with the earth
the earth my only wife
touch me if you can.

244.

Don't worry about the numbers
John Muir told Emerson they keep house by themselves
I teach the interpretation of mirrors
the calculus of skin
how many contacts in a sleeping life
don't wake up for me
for I am sleeping too my music snores
gnats bother the porches of mine ears
how dreadful is the natural
give me the word that flees its thing
let me go to the country music goes to when it fades away
let me live on the ashes of what someone sang.

245.

Where is this *up* I asked you to use me to
a seashell in the sky, grammatical awkwardness
Bruno's cavatina in music someone's bound to die
we all are victims of perceiving
but what image lingers in the dying mind
that is the real question about death
what do we go out with
wearing our curious inherited garments
what symbol nestled in the socket of the throat
so many things to remember only one to carry with me
what is the mind before perceiving
the deep and simple well in which no star shines.

246.

Day of knife angry dreams the crowded train
never any clear way to get home
leaning on the woman till he fell a statue
live in slo-mo with your eyes on fire
Schlomo, the king with a wife for every night
but only one wife for all his days
married to wisdom with a golden lariat
fine-tailed doves fly up into green fronds
all this happens only because you're watching
if we didn't see it wouldn't be
language is the alley of dead kings
lets you speak without opening your mouth.

247.

Walk in the shade disprove the sun
everything has been said before so now we're free
the blue flower is a never-spoken word
the color she bent down to touch became her sky
culture is a long contagion
what can you do with a thought you can't think
the empty parable Satan's answer
if I give you the desert will you give me my emptiness again
all the jewels of the mountain red gravel of the Irrawaddy
I had three homes none of them mine
my wife was mad at me and turned away
for me there was no deeper pit than this.

248.

As if our business is to make our way to hell
only that way find the road to paradise again
who made up all these stories even if they're true
everything that's told is true, is true enough
how much is there to know about you
look into my life to find you
a crack in the windshield makes the sky belong to someone else
you found your way into my arteries I breathe you in
cleansing of the blood miracle of simple prose
grammar of the heart nakedness of any window
we forget the important things so they can happen
an image worn smooth by too much looking.

249.

Where there should be a rose
I write with what I gave you gave me back
all exchanges spiral into one
this is the point the start the target the soul
will you get to the point I am the point
there is no other a minute is my mother
trees look away today don't dry on me
I need your perfect beauty in every line
some people get no older it is a play
retrieve the rain that washes the rose
cistus or labdanum brings the dying back to life
offer this resin in the temple and see what god appears.

250.

To Venus Virgin Mother of the world he wrote
shaky Latin his mind on something else
because nothing is born it all is here forever
love makes us turn our notice to each thing
though things appear to enter the world they were here all along
I like you will you like me back only lovesong a child knows
I will lick your back of course of course
each of us is apt for every need just find the way
if you believe that you'll believe anything
I believe everything because I know
but what he knows he wouldn't say
leaves it to you to find the right word.

251.

Let's do it yesterday
for music's sake the angel facing backwards
there is something of sulfur in the rose
a petal fallen laid along the skin
no other fact can slip past it
natural affinity of rose with flesh
of thorn with mind
the prick of thinking
trickle of blood along the flesh
break the sentence open it will bleed
Scriabin saw his word in color in the sky
a fatal rose that knows so many.

252.

Something true about defilement
wrong tool for the right job
dawn full of feathers fallen
from some legendary bird you never saw
but these things fly their kind is to come
close and touch you while you sleep
you say O my dream but it eats you
disdains your sorry meat
touch defiles
that's why we need it
we come into this dance so pure
no one can remember his father.

253.

No one can read it all the way through
even a single sentence is infinite
a verb is an abyss
he talked about language till it silenced him
humidity abolishes conversation
it is the sea come back to claim us escapees
our local habitation golden trowel round the town
hedges of Donegal all gorse and fuchsia
map the country where my body lives
wherever cold is comfort
half the folk you meet aren't really there
vanish into lush green hills.

254.

The home I never had is you
the god of communication is the god of secrets kept
power of the hermetic axe with two blades
wings on his heels he shows and hides
wherefore set we down words on paper
hoping substance hides what meaning says
every language foreign to a thing
we live in darkness with skins of light
where Hermes is heaven is a letter you can't yet read
spend all your nights deciphering this touch
brutal answer of a cloudless day
it must mean something if it's anything.

255.

Protect this fading image from all the angry gallery
this image I made as me
I am the one who thinks myself to be
bad think bad god
to make this double little world of me and it
make the other be one with me
or one of me or I am none
and where are you in all these trees
leafier this year than ever I've known
after the locust trees blossomed all spring
the basswoods our lindens blossomed high summer
their fragrance fills the house all night when the wind moves.

256.

Once I wanted what would walk through the door
because the guest is god I am an atheist
some pollen fallen from another's tree
grows an absolutely different kind of grain
go inside time to its relenting
suppose I were rain along your spine
would your mind turn rain into someone else
the way not even the weather is personal
smoky breath of an old friend
the taste in someone else's mouth a word is
once you have seen the picture you'll never stop
we have to keep talking to the world to make it go?

257.

The snail shells move in the night like ships
who knows where the copper is that breathes the blood
scratch of a pen on an ancient map
here are the islands of the ancestors
listen and you'll hear your fathers calling
they are praying for the clouds to let them through
they have a name for you a permission
survival of the fastest
dark dark the word gouged in wet sand
they were here before you they're the fathers
you think at first it is the traffic or the birds
but deep in your belly you know better.

258.

The other place than where it is
a gleeful mistake like a dog running away
penny in a pocket sun behind cloud
everything is allowed
when you were a tree I held your leaves for you
when you were ocean I was your waves
the flight attendant listens to the sky
the word is out there just below the plane
when you were a city I did not know how to earn
glamorous ignorance of well-fed tourists
animals are different inside rocks are the same
their brown eyes open in amazement at the snow.

259.

So much to remember and no need to
quiet wise men correct the weather
witchcraft is too natural she said too much about fertility
being fertile is not the point being now is
no one ever did that in my dream before
cloud lift sun back mad at me up there
for I have sought the gods beneath the hill
the little gods who promised nothing but to be
nature is the part of me that's someone else
birdsongs inking lines through trees
always coming back as usual to some flower
I climbed the stairs to where you almost were.

260.

I can't ask for anything amidst so much
the wind is free but rare here a leaf stirs
valley in a valley we live below the map
secret influence streams out around us
that is how it is to be at home
nature was the first mistake: culture the second
there has to be another way
mind slice between the seemings
when I saw the piglets sucking I knew it all was wrong
knew why Ahab turned his body from the sun
why perfect love is always going away.

261.

Happy is a hard thing to hold
there is no money that is not mind
we know so little and it means so much
I keep pretending I'm part of what I say
blue-eyed grass in April deer eat buds in June
roses of what might have been
you'll see the flower pink in their dark eyes
breath finds its way through densest flesh
whisper of the magic jewels inside the clock
starlight over Oahu one more burden to remember
for you it's all a story for you it has no end
silence on the other hand of the sea.

262.

Each line wants to go off somewhere far away
sit there thinking about itself
but we all have noisy neighbors
we lean on one another for the touch
take strength take weakness from each other
even feebleness is reassurance
touch is contagion
but we are here together
tangency is defilement
one line bleeds onto another
you belong to the next thing you say
and to the thing that came before you
then you'll belong to what they finally hear.

263.

Wait for the sun to pry the rose open
then petal by petal take it in the mouth
so delicate it is you have to chew a while
chew to let the taste come in
for these are dark times in personland
animals cull the flowers in the night
animals leave us only the names of things
only things like color shape texture size
things like reason things like belief
that are not things at all only you are
and I am we are the last of the flowers
we grew up before the end of things.

264.

Eloquent darkness of what I didn't bother to think
the things we make up were there already
stories waiting to be believed
amber and lightning waiting to be analyzed
they were all waiting and here we are
the next thing you think will be the truth
the next person you meet will tell it
how easy things are when you say them
a woman in a white robe walking on the sea
believe nothing trust no one revere everyone
that way you fall in love without the fall
that way the apple leaps back to the tree.

265.

Till we have said everything using the same words
music won't leave us alone
children blur the colors in their books
they know that nothing has a line around it
careful signals of a word at peace
let me read my book to the center of the earth
plum trees of Afalon truth of the dragon
a castle in the cool core of the sun
a place previous to transformation
before the legal chemistry begins
a wily anarch in skimpy clothes
as if it all could finally be again.

266.

At a certain point stop looking
at the trees start to read them
the self-planted and the other kind
human implants immigrants our fancies
jade exotics in exurban gardens
three hundred years and still speak foreign
rose of Sharon smokebush lilac
self-taught espontaneos who choose to land
and choose to stay tall and shady and teaching
hue saturation and chroma in their differences
distances between nature and the actual
my father's pine trees on the road to Callicoon.

267.

Where things grow by themselves
that's the scripture for our pilpul
con each leaf and comprehend
this is the Heavenly Academy of what happens
gardens are colonial agribusiness
obliterating the mind's first Text
the uncontrived happenstance of suchness
big words for the tiny weeds between the tiles
I too hurry to obliterate
as if it were a message from the mind before the mind
leave it till you remember what it's saying
a language even the rain speaks just be wet.

268.

Hark to your habit leman
pain is sham as a country is
when countryside is real
so many did to you I mean
as many as sparrows *strouthoi* of her sly chariot
birds are molecules of something very big
isn't that what Empedocles did
you talk all the time about Pythagoras
looking in the mirror is close shave enough
girls taught men poetry by skipping rope
giving hope leaving forever with a lingering smile
naked on tigerback biting the moon.

269.

So much I'd say to you if you were here
but far away I just keep talking
who knows how much the wind will carry
just don't get married the dark woods need you for their own
sweet child of so many mothers
know me as your elder sister
sistrums in our hands and coronets above
we are the only licensed worshippers
we worship shadows of the gods we are
size is a true story and pace is beauty
density of thought a thick saliva sweetish
wets your lips so you can speak the secret word.

270.

Roads reeds spines dawn wind lives inside us
I speak for all of us since I speak alone
you laughed at me across the laundry room
what more does a story need to be
green patterned dress folded on the floor
everything we do together is therapy
use me use me we'll both be clean
how real does it have to be before it is
the pattern was small white flowers
as if spring could take off its clothes still not be naked
it was all about sorting the wash by hand
it was all about waking up at last.

271.

If you carry the dream through the day
a smoky donkey will start to bray
you follow the road to La Borne
those cliffs up to the left we walked it only once
at every house a peaceful dog
signboards modest boast on every villa
we lived in Les Moufflons ten years apart
I didn't understand bird talk in those days
you hadn't taught me the language of bells
and all I knew was bread I clutched it tight
the way a dying man clutches his nurse's thigh
this I know this won't let me go.

272.

I never saw you as you are
you know 'you' means everybody 'I' means nobody
language has a bigger heart than any man
no house but now
a woman at the washing machine
she is the secret ruler of the world
unclad into the changes
fish too plentiful aquarium
always another waiting
the sun came sluggish to this table
a game out there someone else is playing
me too though I sit close-eyed inside.

273.

Anarchic monument
use simple words a child can understand
the littler the word the bigger the spell
say a word to match the skill
the whole business is the people you be with
people who make you more than you
to be a matchmaker of every moment
a Mass-priest of the casual word
and all for you he said and all for me
watching on the subway learn how people read
how they move away from contact
into the strange world this body is.

274.

I want to tell you all the ones I need doctor
because in your glass-wall cabinet you display
one of each essence that pursues my day
dreams are worse when you know who they are
give them to me or make them go away
homeopathic relationships a kiss heals all desire
this is me flouncing out of your office crying on the daybed
this is the cabin boy on a steamer that sank
this is the girl with the paper flower in her hair
resemblances are terrible isn't it enough to have one of a thing
must her shadow pass through every door
can't I make you stop looking at me that way.

275.

I lost the word at dawn I knew in sleep
poor me a hundred thousand other words around but that one gone
agrestic agnostic arthritic aesthetic
but still the mercy monument went up
trapezoidal in outline a frustrated pyramid
built of all the shadows I have ever tried to reify
a junk heap halfway to the moon yet shapely withal
experiences change from other eyes
long after only by its cover can you tell a book
I will take a net and go down to the little stream
and let the shadow of its meshwork float on quick water
and no one will be wounded by my music.

276.

There is a cello at the bottom of the spine
that is how Europe got here so deep
why Tiepolo painted the actual sky above an ordinary me
we are embedded in what we thought we knew
people greeking language under my hands
I'm not talking culture I'm talking neurology
the complex music of our simple meat
lift up the manhole covers see who we are
cables and sewers information overflow
I am the conduit of the impersonal
can't forget Nora splashing surf at Rockaway   *NW*
so much the worse for me.

277.

On the glass face of the device the window birds reflected
pass over the house so short is music
music is an accident happened to the air
ergo bird bassoon the bells of Judson Church
but mostly this little mirror in my hand
shows the arcane image of each sound
what we look like when we hear the cardinal chirp
what the crow means in soaring without sound
over my poor house! personal again
the complicated negotiations in a dream
a wise old counterman without a word
pointed to fried chicken that's the piece for you.

278.

So when everything fits into one thing
the voice of that one thing is heard
the grace you give me let me tell you everything
the slow highway to Toronto roadhouse on the lake
the crowded yellow bed in Montreal
the waterfall in Assam
all of these could be my name
but comedy is finished the epic begins
my cousin's will in probate lyric as a lotus
grandfather looked like Wallace Stevens but he could smile
haven't I followed Dante step by step
if your ears are clean you will hear my Tuscan lisp.

279.

It scares me when I get personal
like those dreams you're half naked
we are never fully undone though
even death is only half the dance
so I can tell you everything
till I have nothing left
and your skin will still be cool on the coverlet
and sleep will tell me some more lies
the kind I can live with
there is no socialist remedy for this situation
except do everything for the other guy
if you can ever find anybody really different.

280.

Flute in the nineteenth century the phone is ringing
yes I am guilty of everything
all I did all I do was this
birds walking on the roof just like the French poem
but the sea is very far
one arm of it though strikes through the land
the River North into a different skin
as far as a ship can sail against the grain
for this is a wooden world and I am wooden too
no one hears the suffering of trees
so caught up with using them leaf shade and timber
and these are my leaves mesdames I leave for you.

281.

Under the tunic the wound begins to bleed
losing the city was worth it we get to find it again
we had to set the image free
with blood I mark crisscross on this stone
nearby an altar chiseled by no iron
defiled only by a word it speaks
through my palms the rock talks up my arms
this was the first stone in the world
jihad against the unbelieving emptiness
fight for the vibrant hollow of the spacious mind
blood was meant to be the secret ink
writing the sutra of reality deep inside your frame.

282.

The devil saw through you
every raster of your busy soul
the fight at sundown
miracle at the mothergate
where all sorts of light spill in
it was you standing there before the world
so much for unheard music
even understanding, what good is that
are you just an alderman of saying so
a princeling of improvised despair?
legitimacy tree, let the light in!
spirit can make use of even me.

283.

But what if it's all wrong
every few minutes a boy comes by and takes an apple
you never know when he's coming
you'll never know how many apples you have
it turns out the sea really is made of ink
and we are the scripture that it wrote
are you ready for me yet to read and leap
the bull calf sprinkled with wine and daisies
offered living to the Place he stands in
grazes and lifts to gore the trembling light
live forever is what he says it says
a sutra that has soared up then fallen from our whys.

284.

Get your work done before the sun comes up
how the day curls up at your feet
time changes and you stay the same
for once your skin fits you
suddenly there are flowers on the rose of Sharon
you start remembering all manner of pink things
the day wakes up again and bites your ankle
memory is the thief of time
rub your lantern bright and go down the cave
lick the pretty pictures off the wall
that's what eyes are for you think
those bottomless wells where the light gets lost.

285.

Life stops at any moment but the story goes on
that's what's wrong with it, this imaginary present tense
weirder than any future hold me in your hands
because I was war and got over it or praised the seen
read the clay tablets of Gilgamesh with your fingers
there is no scholarship but the waking heart
for saying is all and thinking is few
those dim magistrates dismiss all evidence
if you believe your eyes you'll believe anything
I'm an agnostic when it comes to me
I speak to the simplest things because they answer me
the question I really meant for you.

286.

Smash the tablets at the gate
to speak in the tongues of all of you
I need to answer what you do not ask
isn't that what *polis* is for
the heads to hang crowns on and laurel wreaths
rhapsodic recitation of the obvious
smooth as religion
but it's hard in summer when the gods are far
we linger in our bodies no more sense than the day's news
now I put on my father's green coat
and speak another language taught by the mirror
seen through tears as he went away.

287.

When it caught me I was the meadow
but we all have a right to that green place
where every flower is a telephone to hell
because the colors we see so different are the mind of somewhen else
far away right beneath our feet
or did you Lady beneath our skin
where the shining trumpets blaze drums dare to touch
is it there or is it there
of course the land I mean is someone else
right here if only I'd stop talking
if only you would speak
saddest of all songs white-throated sparrows'.

288.

Coming to feeling
no one knows what a word means in the mouth of the other
this is axiomatic not even the skin knows
who touched me? I felt the power reaching out from me
touch heals but who or whom
what does the skin know of touch
intention or accident love or scorn the earth is blue
that's all we knew
enough to be a pirate in a sea of talk
stand by your word until it falls
then bury it in language that loud café
among full cups, church the most godly.

289.

Nothing is likely to end
the intellect is just now blossoming
should I hand over to it this work of saying
she is easier to read but harder to understand
all touch dissolves in color
color crystalizes into sound
a sound you mistake for a word
rain on marble steps slippery as poetry
but it isn't raining it isn't anywhere
the word you think you heard unlocks your memory
everything you remember escapes and runs away
leaving you free at last alone with your own meaning.

290.

Who made me feel like this a life ago?
deer eat the lower buds only up top are new roses
that's history for you, a bird bounces off a window
falls, shakes itself and flies away
even without a leaf there would be weather
the saddest thing a city loses is the sky
show me a cloud I'll show you paradise
dissolve all that is solid life breathes out
bring together in one word all that is fugitive
then swallow that word and live forever
your breath will always smell of it
enough to teach millions when you kiss.

291.

Successiveness dissolves in *klang*
all the notes played at once of what will be a 'song'
use the simplest word for it
a word now sick with commercial implication
song as commodity is a root of war
copyright is blasphemy
all of these words are yours to begin with
I just got in the way on their way to you
shall we end at the Milvian Bridge
where they began to confuse Christ with Cæsar
o throw that denarius away his face is in the sky
no his face is your face when you wake up.

292.

That was good kyning they'll never say of me
I lost Cæsar on the way to France
a slim-hipped nation on a crowded bus
Europe is always on the march I want to sit still
buying a dictionary brought me closer to love
I was so young I believed in what I read in what I said
even if I didn't believe a word of what it said
I was a boy with a penknife looking for the bark of a tree
to carve my initials and find out who I was
the trees were quick in those days and I was slow
so I remembered music Mahler mostly
and pretended it was you talking to just me.

293.

So much for me, life begins when you forget
and live by feeling through the world of will
that angry place of plastic and aluminum
commonest elements made hard to hurt
so feeling is your best blade young man
keep silence till you get to say it
spoken silence is the richest meat
and nourishes the clarity inside
all those layers of you till I get to me
and always always the other way round
Leipzig the fugue trapped in the organ
I opened the creaking door and let it out.

294.

Old pens old friends the given always gets
hand it to me we say and hand it surely is
weather of a distant city breath of your mouth
transhuman rhapsody suck on your finger now
o you everything you beast of a million leaves
make me listen to your touch
also spoke sorrow after joy to mingle
red sky at evening leave your grieving
all you lost is safe in Amitabha's glowing land
it is good to console better to unmind the sorrow
who are you to lose to feel to grieve
answer me that you Trinity scholar and rejoice.

295.

I'm translating back into my mother tongue
what I heard in the high mountains
what I learned under the hill
earth gods and mind lords and me in between
a haggard buffoon with a bottle of ink
o sail me to your island ever after
pillow me with stillness till the fever eases
then I'll take hold of autumn skies
and bring them onward with a sheen of rain
to cool the counsel of an angry world
gets hotter by the day as if all scriptures
give us one mandate to conquer and kill.

296.

Religion is to dance as prison to the Constitution
the underside the got-it-wrong the social trap the money
when all the great ones said go to yourself in the empty place
quiet room or vacant tree
sit there silent till you know
know enough at least to help and how
and know that we all need you
yes I need you to be, tree behind you now
you walk around the world
hinting how to take the pain away
we make for each other and ourselves
now put that in your organ and play on.

297.

I am not the only one who I am
the others need me too
the lighthouse turns out to be the moon
raspberry bushes replete with thorn
make me doubt the sweet real things
flesh and its discontents, pink tongues
on suburban buses o I have lived too much
too little time and bring it all to you
that word again the queen of implications
sparrow hawks and midnight hens
you taught me all the names of birds
I've had to do my forgetting all alone.

298.

Need the cool of midnight in our clothes
birds in roses fairies all the straight of us
I am understanding all standing under
mother-earth mother-sea mother-me
the dream explained, the dream is always
always California beyond the mountains on a foreign sea
"grew up on Atlantic, hard to believe the Pacific's made of water"
head full of the fumes of Oregon laurel
a naked friend a deer skull on Tamalpais
before religion and all the rest of politics
before stories before music before words
curves of lettuce blades of rocket and moist cress.

299.

I pretend a purely human genome
but we know better we have weather
ta metarsia weather is our father hence Jove
all the fables of father sky mean this
be made pregnant by the moment
we only pretend to have a history
is samsara the same as Time?
does the blood ever take a vacation?
sunlight is the only answer heaven gives
so look elsewhere for *les droits de l'homme*
a barque imperiled on calm seas
a wind straight from the center of the earth.

300.

Something like a breeze through people green as trees
this is your moment mother
before the flowers come and go
a life of gentlest waiting
like the hibiscus for its bee
a bird will do, anything I can say you to
and love a little while, the mild
adultery of objects fondled then set free
there is a moment in the stillest things
we learned in the sacred tedium of Sunday Mass
eloquent silences between the words
when the priest stopped mumbling and held Something in his hands.

301.

But God is more personal than sex
when the outside and the inside are the same
a horse you never heard of comes rushing from the mountains
the comfort of enough against the ecstasy of more
o horse you cry I will not ride today
but he thinks otherwise and there you are aloft
the two of you above the hills beast and human
who knows which is which a fable no one ever tells
vanishing in blue distances song fading
nobody knows nobody knows I hear the dearest voice
laughing at the effort I put into doing nothing
a snowstorm of images around a freezing child.

302.

You want to translate Homer I want to write him
all new all over again all shining and no war
no more war and the pale cheeks of men
pierced by no bronze prong and no fire
walks up and down the corpse and the hymn
that grieves for Linos turns into the Ode to Joy
a cliché has no memory it plugs a leak
even Homer nods so I can snore as well
and pour the beauty of Helen and Diomedes and Kassandra
back into the ordinary dance of day
and we will know each other in that company
proud abashed a little silly full of soul.

303.

They must know their bodies well
since they have nothing else to know
knowing never stops
it's time to come back from the underworld
just as I am just as I am
backwards always is everything
no age but awareness
give us our animal back
sex is an accident on the road to truth
take off your shoes for this is holy ground
the feeling that your body is
there is no other world than this.

304.

A poem is guided meditation
mild propulsion of the written world
when it stops the process it launched sails on
knowing the mind
clear light between the names of things
between the things
so.ma the bright between
the new the fresh the uncontrived
your mind finds by itself
sacred absence in the core of you
all the holiness and shadows pass
maidens and heroes and sunlight on the sea.

305.

So little said and so much waking
salt meadow hay best mulch men say
I've managed to know nothing but what I can speak
the van is at the door it's all just weather
sitting here alone with my hibiscus tree
the written evidence tells against my life
my father by the cellar door painting grey
everything waits for us below
an image worthy of your eye
the end of the pagan world was the end of the world
nothing learned nothing lost
I marvel at the emptiness of me.

306.

So it can mean a little or a lot
a billboard on a vacant lot is all my Hollywood
and see behind it how the lovers chance
it would be Ancient Greek if it had a goat
but wisdom does not wear a coat
the afternoon is longer than the night
or so the bird explained
a language half sound half color
all things intersect in you
all the silken raptures of the couch
rainstorm in the desert
from great pain some red flowers after.

307.

Lost endowment will update on deathbed
signed but unwitnessed the hospital in flames
the law was born to make us kind we pray
but every river has its crocodile the teeth of our detail
Lauretta grieves for babbo Dante snickers in hell
death itself is the gift they leave the living
a holy absence with some names in it
images and places green coat Swan Lake Narrowsburg
give the little I have to the many
Multiplication of the Loaves and Fish you do by leaving
these chips and chances were my working mind
here dear friends my baseless box of trinkets.

308.

One or two more miracles a bird on its bush
a mountain then another one who are you fooling
is all philosophy a consolation what else could it be or do
in the shadow of Plato some folk pierced through thinking
maybe or am I five thousand miles west of where it was
a wordless opening through behavior to the ordinary mind
effortless spun gold from neutron stars set this bird in flight again
without even the intention to be, is
flagship of feeling through tumultuous seas
to the quiet story of a sandy beach a shell upon it
which held to your good ear says the primal word
before your witless fingers reach for something else.

309.

So we're back with love and not much else
greatest of all seemings unless you fall in it
we're back with love it springs us forward
into the kindness of our only hope the yellow of the rose
where no one lives and all love rises
to spell the billion stories that we tell
all their theology old comfy car
Packard or Panhard on its way through the sky
all roads lead to home
that's all you need to have
a little knowledge and some gasoline
smile brother you're almost there.

310.

Spark that made water come from hydrogen and oxygen
someone had to throw the switch
is it you who look at me oddly sometimes
as if surprised to find me there beside you
who could the spark be but the other
we come from ocean but where did ocean come from
who else is ripening down there now
ready to crawl out as we did and take our place
asking questions of the howling wind
playing their flutes in the desert
and like us always trying to remember
where we came from and why.

311.

Accidental purposes of Delta music
on that day women chase men or seem to
they shall handle texts and not be harmed thereby
they shall preach the good news without knowing it
old battleships with concave prows
plow into tropic harbors bring truth home
tapa cloth and Charlie Chan and Maori skin
everything written was written to be forgotten
forgotten deep into you and ripen there
nasturtiums a little peppery in her salad
mud fights in Oregon knishes on Pitkin
if you think these are random think again.

312.

Children in the cornfield who are you now
furtive actions in the furrows
who knows what eating really does
two children lying side by side
hieroglyph of the space left between them
every relationship makes its own sign
world a museum unknown curator about whom we fantasize
theology philosophy history and baffling pre-dawn dreams
where we are always in a far-off city always trying to get home
so this planet must itself be the distant town
the stewardess won't let me on the plane
must be the fiery angel she drives me off with an ear of corn.

313.

She was in him all the time
Rosa peregrina pressed between the pages
so much talk the morning mower
break into an art beyond commodity
you pilgrim rose that took his hand
led him to color alone and left him there
while she herself stepped up inside him
castle of palaver beauty counts
on one finger the ruby of the setting sun
we live again because we mistake
this art too beyond the financiers
life belongs really only to the poor.

314.

Poverty is permanent is to live in a physical world
endlessly interdependent dependent on each puff of breath
each stone you stand on your will contingent on the molecular
even if you think you're not just mirror neurons
just the habit of acquiring speech
because it doesn't lead anywhere
it perdures or seems to as long as you do
the world has never abandoned anyone
up to you to leave the world
naked towards the riches of the unconceived
I love you she said despite all this I tell
oiled wrestlers grappling with the moment seems.

315.

I can't help it if it tells the truth
the weather's like that, breeze and knees
there is waiting to be done because the world
subways are so old-fashioned
we are children when we go down there
blue light in the Clark Street tunnel
the hardest is to be now at all
broken branches where the deer browsed
I think of winter and of Scamander
the river rising to rebuke us
the gods of everything for everything's a god
not us though we're on the other side of that.

❡

316.

In the completion things get in the way
until it occurs to her they *are* the way
then she leads me to it and you too
the other side of everything and here we are
I have to talk like this I am a voice
only what we say counts not what we do
he said and climbed the rain-drenched slope
into a Chinese dream he never wanted
why all those fan-fold books peonies and lexicons
of course he wanted to go there provided *there* was here
only the voice moved drifting over the hospital gardens
old man weeping on the marble steps.

317.

So what if her skirt is made of flowers
his skin was made of ocean
people grow old with what they hold
all that holding hurts
pain of a violin how can I sing with something in my head
the pale arm that calms me so many nights
all a step away from mania
where does the sound come from you rub on your strings
consider the pain of all I give you
is all forgiving blue light of the other
fills the whole body the way sound fills the ears
only this and nothing else.

318.

I hear voices in the white noise of the window fan
midnight conversation of the atmosphere
such tender images to select your message
I thought it said and why not listen
an image is a wound subject to change decay
but somehow lasts forever
I can't get you out of my mind we say
then a chickadee hops on the porch rail and chases you away
an image silences an image
morphs into it as grass is green
but no two blades the same, never the same color
I take what comfort I can from the differences.

319.

The bowl of night beleaguered me
then airless dawn we read about in books
written by frustrated selfish young men
there is always air enough for women
even poor Salome here I can breathe! but night
had other plans and other selfish men
the one who wouldn't kiss her one who killed for kissing
o it is strange to be a woman in this world
to have made all this then see it turn against you
boy by boy until the mean old men enslave you
I wish I could do something to change or help
but I'm a habit man mechanical like all the rest.

320.

Long footnote here to show the primacy of Eve
but you've heard it all already and don't believe
but I believe I believe in everything
I'm just a man on a raft after all
and you are the sea where else could we be going
around and around on Ocean River, be Other
synovial fluid the river inside us
we link with Other only when we drink or weep
there is a butterfly but where is my cellphone
banal be me Beatrice! he said and clomb
up the scree slopes of vocabulary to a wordless crest
and rested there eased by cool mist he thought.

321.

A troll is not a little thing it's a living stone
a stone that knows how to move
a stone with hands and only the *huldra* tames him
or so I read in a book I wrote
I found it on my phone faces made of shadows
light itself is made of their soft fur
they're all around us their breath the thunder
all summer I've been translating from the birds
now who will be my dragoman
and guide you cleanly through my cloying text?
it's done already! you've read and understood!
what else is there to tell but how it sounds?

322.

All that's missing is the rain of gold
on Danae's outspread self, the blue flower
clinging to your fingertips the crow calling loud
right overhead to tell me what's what
the time has come he says *kairos*
like a glee or a gospel anything you choose
long as it has a tune in it
the watchman on the roof stirs in his sleep
the trees wake up and tremble at that song
you wear your clothes woven from the stars
I know who you are but with all
my talk that's the one word I won't say.

323.

And if it rains we say some other thing
and if the sparrows drown out timid raindrops
there'll be some peace at last in this cartoon
forgive me my investigations a bee has to live
the drones hum around the hive those artists boy-band poets
I'm just the wrong kind a man I couldn't find
honey in a honey jar how strange the world is
all contents and containers and a bird going by
knowing no more than we and no less
voices of the cyclists wheeling past
chatting loud as if they're standing still
the slender miracle of mind we all can hear.

324.

I climbed in winter up Glastonbury Tor
stood in the ruins of St. Michael's Chapel
peered up through the roofless tower to watch
the original star from which we fell
you and I slept together on the Hill of Tara
peaceful in cool summer
right beneath the Stone of Destiny
we live our little times apart
Himalayas blue flowers too
where is there for us to think
but this half-acre hot summer
birdsong almost too many leaves
very green, this place, here.

325.

No lingering slumbery rubato flaunted coda—
without slowing down it simply stops
Stefano Greco plays Bach's unfinished contrapunctus
that way, he has a theory I never understand
but I agree silence is the best philosophy
those empty minutes that we long to touch
I fill them here with ambrosia
a sappy word that means in Greek what does not die
life, that limitless cliché
o love me as much as I love you
you can do it if anybody can
you are the only one who understands.

CPSIA information can be obtained
at www.ICGtesting.com
Printed in the USA
FSOW01n1831270816
24217FS

9 780997 371505